mastering the
middlegame

ANGUS DUNNINGTON

First published 2001 by Everyman Publishers plc, formerly Cadogan Books plc, Gloucester Mansions, 140A Shaftesbury Avenue, London WC2H 8HD

British Library Cataloguing-in-Publication Data
A catalogue record for this book is available from the British Library.

ISBN 1 85744 228 8

Distributed in North America by The Globe Pequot Press, P.O Box 480, 246 Goose Lane, Guilford, CT 06437-0480.

All other sales enquiries should be directed to Everyman Chess, Gloucester Mansions, 140A Shaftesbury Avenue, London WC2H 8HD
tel: 020 7539 7600 fax: 020 7379 4060
email: dan@everyman.uk.com
website: www.everyman.uk.com

To Sardine

EVERYMAN CHESS SERIES (formerly Cadogan Chess)
Chief Advisor: Garry Kasparov
Commissioning editor: Byron Jacobs

Typeset and edited by First Rank Publishing, Brighton
Production by Book Production Services
Printed and bound in Great Britain by The Cromwell Press Ltd., Trowbridge, Wiltshire

Contents

Introduction

This book is designed to help the student of the game sit at the board with more confidence, armed with an appreciation of a number of important practical aspects of the middlegame. Obviously the very constraints of a book make it impossible to provide any kind of 'complete' guide, not least because the middlegame is a mass of uncharted territory. However, the same cannot be said of opening theory, for example, where we have the luxury of exact sequences of moves, while even endings can be studied precisely, with many situations analysed exhaustively.

The middlegame, in fact, is a cruel sea that separates the relatively safe, dry land of opening and ending. As soon as the pieces drift from the posts allotted to them by theory they become our responsibility, and we are more or less left to our own devices as to how to best treat them.

With this in mind I have accumulated a selection of practical examples that can be seen in tournament halls everywhere, with an emphasis on how this or that factor might be applied in our own experience. Rather than make an overview of general rules and advice I have concentrated on mainly positive themes, ranging from outright attack to strong defence. In other words, the areas of the middlegame we investigate might have positional, psychological and attacking significance or they could feature a specific piece, but they are all linked by the common denominator that is a better understanding of the game.

Chapter One

Attacking the King

As this book is aimed at addressing some of the more crucial aspects of the game, none is more important than the king. In this chapter we concentrate on how strong players go about attacking the enemy king when it is still in the centre (often a somewhat risky situation in the middlegame!) and when one side castles long and the other castles short. Both these scenarios arise from a host of openings and defences, so playing through the examples carefully should be of considerable use regardless of your repertoire. We will also discuss the importance of eliminating key defenders (a theme often overlooked at club level), and the importance of staying alert to aggressive possibilities in ostensibly calm positions.

The King in the Centre

Game 1
□ **Kallai** ■ **Pinter**
Balatonbereny 1995

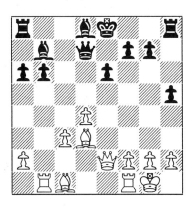

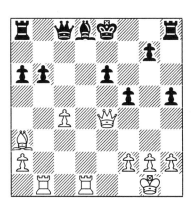

Diagram 1
Can Black castle kingside?

Diagram 2
Black's king is wide open

After earlier committing himself with ...h7-h5 (to chase away White's queen from g4) Black can no longer consider castling. Consequently White prepares action in the centre.

16 c4 Qxd4

Faced with an unpleasant choice, Black accepts the hot d-pawn rather than see it come to d5. The alternative 16...h4 17 d5 h3 18 g3 0-0 19 Qe4 g6 20 Qg4 simply drops the h-pawn.

17 Rd1!

Taking up a threatening stance on another centre file and putting the question to the queen.

17...Qd7

After 17...Qc5 18 Be3 (18 Rb3!?) 18...Qc6 19 f3 0-0 Black castles but
the h5-pawn will still prove problematic and, in the meantime, White
can switch flanks with 20 c5! b5 21 a4 Qc8 22 axb5 axb5 23 Bxb5 Bc6
24 Rd6, when Black is under pressure.

18 Be4 Qc8

After 18...Qc7 19 c5! Bxe4 20 Qxe4 Rb8 21 cxb6 Rxb6 22 Qa4+ Ke7
(22...Qc6 23 Qxc6+ Rxc6 24 Rb8 Ke7 25 Ba3+) 23 Rxb6 Qxb6 24 Bg5+!
the game is over, while 19...b5 20 a4! clearly favours White. Hoping to
alleviate the pressure with a queen sacrifice is futile: 18...Qxd1+ 19
Qxd1 Bxe4 and now White continues the theme with 20 Qa4+! b5 21
cxb5 Bxb1 22 b6+, e.g. 22...Kf8 23 Qc6 Rb8 24 Qd6+, or 22...Ke7 23
Ba3+ Kf6 24 b7 Rb8 25 Qf4+ etc.

19 Ba3

By activating his final piece White reminds his opponent of his plight,
keeping Black's king stranded in the centre. Note that White threatens the deadly 20 Rxd8+! Kxd8 21 Qd2+ Ke8 22 Qd6.

19...Bxe4

19...Bc7 fails to slow White down in view of 20 Qb2! f6 21 Qb4 etc.
Black can also eliminate the other bishop pair first with 19...Be7,
when 20 Bxe7 Kxe7 21 Rxb6 Bxe4 22 Qxe4 Rb8 23 Rbd6 allows White
– who entertains ideas of 24 Qd4 or 24 Qh4 – to maintain the pressure.

20 Qxe4 f5 (Diagram 2) 21 Rxd8+!

The beginning of the next phase – Black's king is suddenly friendless.

21...Kxd8 22 Qh4+!

Not 22 Qd4+? Qd7 23 Qxb6+ Ke8 when Black's king returns to base
but enjoys considerable safety. Kallai's selection, on the other hand,
continues the flushing out process.

22...Kc7

Blocking with 22...g5 rules out a second block after 23 Qd4+ because
the rook is hanging.

23 Qd4!!

Excellent control from White. How many players would rush into 23
Qe7+? Qd7 24 Bd6+ Kc8, when White's attack fizzles out?

**WARNING: Beware of automatic checks when attacking the king –
this might help the defender find a safe(r) haven.**

23...b5

Black cannot avoid the loss of the b-pawn and the subsequent removal of the final layer of defence. Other tries are 23...Qd7 24 Qxb6+ Kc8 25 Bd6, with the deadly threat of the check on b8, and 23...Rb8 24 Qd6+ Kb7 25 Rxb6+ Ka7 26 Bc5! Qxc5! 27 Rxa6+ Kb7 28 Qxc5 Kxa6, which is a brave attempt but leaves White in charge after 29 Qa3+ Kb6 30 Qd6+ Ka5 31 h4, thanks to the weaknesses on e6, g7 and h5.

24 cxb5 Qd7 25 b6+ Kd8 26 Be7+! (Diagram 3)

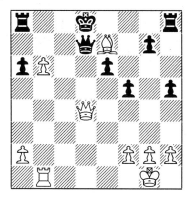

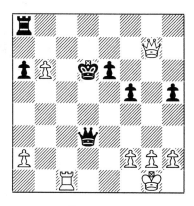

Diagram 3
The final attack begins

Diagram 4
It's all over

The final humiliation forces Black's king to limp back to e8, which is where the troubles began!

26...Ke8

26...Kxe7 27 Qxg7+.

27 Qxg7 Qd3

27...Qxe7 28 Qxh8+ Qf8 29 Qxh5+ is decisive.

28 Qxh8+ Kxe7 29 Qg7+ Kd6 30 Rc1 1-0 (Diagram 4)

Black does not give his opponent the satisfaction of meeting 30...Rc8 with 31 Qc7+! for another hit at Black's king.

Game 2
☐ **Karpov** ■ **Timman**
Jakarta 1993

This time the central king seems less of a problem because the position is reasonably closed, and there is the small matter of the legendary Karpov sitting on White's side of the board! However, a king in the centre is a king in the centre, and we should always be alert for the possibility of exploitation.

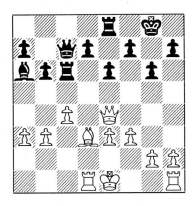

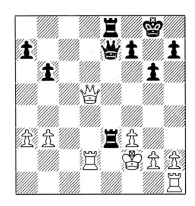

Diagram 5
White's king is not yet safe

Diagram 6
Black controls the e-file!

19...d5!

If we were asked to suggest an interesting move for Black in the diagram position the text would not be a difficult move to find. Whether or not it is actually sound is another matter, but the trick is to recognise when such a possibility is appropriate.

TIP: With a king in the centre try to make yourself aware of how one or more centre files can be opened.

20 cxd5 Bxd3 21 Qxd3

21 Rxd3 Rc1+ is rather awkward for White.

21...exd5 22 Kf2

Now 22 0-0 Rc3 23 Qxd5 Rexe3 sees Black net a pawn for no compensation. Anticipating exchanges, White prefers to have his king ready. Unfortunately for Karpov, his king is not yet safe.

22...Rc3 23 Qxd5 Rcxe3 24 Rd2 Qe7! (Diagram 6)

Lining up all the major pieces on a single file tends to cause the opponent problems, and here Black threatens to push his rook to e1. White cannot do the same on the d-file in view of (25 Rhd1) 25...Qh4+, hence Karpov's next, desperate looking advance.

25 Kg3 Rxb3! 26 a4

26 Qxb3 Qg5+.

26...Rb4 27 Rd4 Rxd4 28 Qxd4 Qg5+ 29 Kh3 Re2

If 'good positions tend to play themselves', then poor positions often become worse, and the latest blow is a fitting culmination of Black's initial strike.

30 Rg1 Qh5+ 31 Kg3 Qg5+

We can forgive Timman for repeating here!

32 Kh3 Rd2 33 Qc3 Ra2 34 Qd4 h6

Cruel.

35 Qc4 Qh5+ 36 Kg3 Qe5+ 37 Kh3 Rd2 38 Qh4 Qf5+ 39 Kg3

Trading queens leads to the loss of the a4-pawn and the game. The text hastens the end.

39...g5 40 Qxh6 Qf4+ 0-1

The sight of Karpov's king so utterly exposed only ten moves after an ostensibly safe position should serve as a warning to us all.

TIP: In the middlegame stage, if your king is still in the centre for no good reason, it might be time to consolidate.

Game 3
☐ Baburin ■ Saidy
Los Angeles 1997

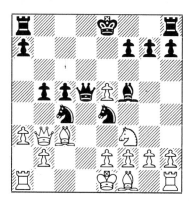

Diagram 7
Where should the black king go?

Diagram 8
Black has a decisive breakthrough

It is fair to say that Black looks threatening, with White's king – unlike its opposite number – stranded on e1. The question is, can Black exploit his opponent's rather cramped situation?

16...0-0-0!!

At first glance this is an odd choice of lodging for Black's king compared with the kingside, the lack of available protection being the most obvious factor. However, by castling long Black has a practically 'free' move in that the rook is brought directly to the d-file, thus ruling out the desired 17 Rd1? in view of the fork after multiple trades on d1 and ...Nxf2+. Consequently Black exerts maximum pressure, correctly judging that his own king is quite secure on c8 – even after the capture of the b5-pawn – since White's forces are not appropriately positioned to benefit from the holes on the queenside.

 TIP: Weigh up the 'pros' and 'cons' of an aggressive move when attacking the enemy king – if your opponent is placed under great pressure at the cost of minor inconvenience, then don't be afraid to bite the bullet.

17 Qxb5!?

Obviously Black is ready for this but taking the pawn looks like the best practical chance for White. Instead 17 e3 Nxe3! 18 Qxd5 Nc2+! cuts across White's hopes of simplification. An interesting variation is 17 Rc1 a6! 18 g3 Rhe8 19 Bg2 Ne3 20 Qxd5 Nxg2+ 21 Kf1 Ne3+! 22 fxe3 Bh3+ 23 Ke1 Rxd5 when the queens are off but White's king continues to be a burden.

17...Nxc3 18 bxc3 Nxe5

Black has designs on the e-file, too. Otherwise he might consider the equally direct 18...Nd2 19 Qb2 Nb3 20 c4 Qxc4 21 Ra2 Qd5, when 22 Nd2 Nxd2 23 Qxd2 Qxe5 24 Qb2 Qxb2 25 Rxb2 Rd6, with the simple plan of reminding White that the king is still awkwardly placed on e1, favours Black.

19 Qb2 Rhe8 20 Nxe5 Rxe5 21 e3

21 c4!? deserves a try now that Black's queen is tied to the defence of the rook.

21...c4! 22 Qa2 Be6 23 Rg1 Qa5 24 Rc1 Qc5! 25 Be2 (Diagram 8) Rxe3!

Suddenly, thanks to the fork after 26 fxe3 Qxe3, Black has a rook on each open, centre file, the latest capture introducing a decisive pin.

26 Qb2 Bg4! 27 Rc2

White's position is beginning to crumble now that the key e3-pawn has fallen. After 27 f3 Rxf3 and 27 fxe3 Qxe3 28 Rf1 Bxe2 the game is over.

27...Re7 28 Rf1 Bf5 29 Rd2 Rxd2 30 Kxd2 Rxe2+! 31 Kxe2 Bd3+ 32 Kf3

32 Ke1 Qe5+.

32...Bxf1 0-1

While it is true that White could have defended better, the cold logic behind the straightforward 16...0-0-0 is worth remembering. Black was not prepared to let his opponent's king out of his sight and thus found the most effective, ruthless means with which to bring both rooks to the centre as quickly as possible.

Castling on Opposite Wings

Game 4
□ **Krasenkow** ■ **Barcenilla**
Subic Bay 1998

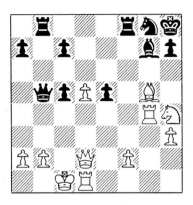

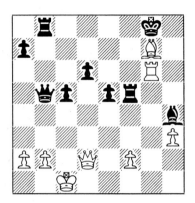

Diagram 9
Which attack will be quicker?

Diagram 10
Black's king has been stripped

In Diagram 9 both sides look menacing indeed, with Black's pressure on the b-file the most obvious feature. Meanwhile, on the other flank, Black's king is not without support, but White is able to quickly alter the circumstances and thus deflect attention away from the b2-pawn.

21 Ng6+! hxg6 22 Rh4+ Nh6 23 Bxh6 Rf5 24 d6!?

24 b3 is Krasenkov's suggestion, simply taking some of the sting out of Black's queen and rook. With the text White is not concerned about the b-pawn, opting instead to continue the assault.

24...cxd6 25 Rg1

Now that both d6 and d5 are available to the queen White brings his final piece into the attack. Tempting but inaccurate is 25 Bxg7+ Kxg7 26 Qh6+ Kf7 27 Qh7+ Kf8, e.g. 28 Qh8+? Ke7 29 Rh7+ Ke6 etc.

25...Bf6 26 Rxg6! Bxh4?

It is easier to miscalculate when an extra rook is involved! Black does better to insert 26...Qf1+, e.g. 27 Kc2 Bxh4 28 Bg7+ Kg8 and the presence of the queen on f1 is a vital difference to what happens in the game: 29 Bf6+? Kf7 30 Rg7+ Ke6 31 Re7+ Kxf6 32 Qxd6+ Kg5 33 Rg7+ Kf4 34 Rg4+ (34 Qd2+ Ke4 35 Qe3+ Kd5) 34...Kf3 35 Qd5+ Kxf2 when White has nothing better than perpetual check. An improvement is 29 Bxe5+ 29...Kf7 30 Rg7+ Ke8 (30...Kf8 31 Qxd6+) 31 Rg8+ Rf8 (31...Kf7 32 Qd5+) 32 Rxf8+ Kxf8 33 Qxd6+ Kf7 34 Qd5+, since

Black will ultimately suffer after 34...Ke8 (34...Kg6 35 Qe6+) 35 Bxb8 (35 Qc6+ Kf7 36 Qf3+) 35...Qxf2+ (35...Qe2+ 36 Qd2 Qc4+ 37 Kd1) 36 Kb3 Bf6 37 Be5 Qe3+ (37...c4+ 38 Ka4 Qc2+ 39 Kb5) 38 Bc3 Bxc3 39 bxc3 Qxh3 40 Kc4, or 34...Kf8 35 Qf3+! Kg8 (35...Ke7 36 Bxb8 Qc4+ 37 Qc3 Qe2+ 38 Qd2 Qc4+ 39 Kd1) 36 Bxb8 Qc4+ 37 Kd1 Qd4+ (37...Qf1+ 38 Kd2) 38 Ke1 Qb4+ 39 Kf1 Qxb8 40 Qg4+ Kf8 41 Qxh4 Qxb2 42 Qc4, White having a winning ending in both cases.

27 Bg7+ Kg8 (Diagram 10) 28 Bf6+!

In our initial position Black's king enjoyed considerable protection yet now the closest pieces are white. However, with material invested and the b2-pawn under fire, it is imperative that White is able to demonstrate that his opponent's king is indeed in his grasp.

28...Kf7 29 Rg7+ Ke6 30 Re7+ Kxf6 31 Qxd6+ Kg5 32 Rg7+ Kf4 33 Rg4+ Kf3 34 Qd5+ Ke2

If we compare the position after 34...Kxf2 with the one reached in the note to 26...Qf1+, there the queen provided necessary help. Here White has 35 Qg2+ Ke3 36 Re4+ followed by immediate mate.

35 Qd1+! Kxf2 36 Qg1+ Ke2 37 Re4+ Kf3 38 Qe3+ 1-0

38...Kg2 39 Rg4+ Kh2 40 Qg1+ Kxh3 41 Qg2 is mate. White's relentless endeavours to strip his opponent's king deserved to succeed.

TIP: With opposite sides castling try to stay in the driving seat, concentrating on keeping up the momentum and therefore denying the opponent the opportunity to strike back.

Game 5
□ **Lugovoi** ■ **Goloshchapov**
Moscow 1998

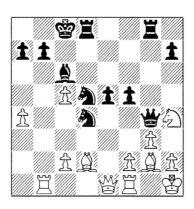

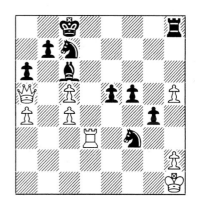

Diagram 11
How can White's king be opened up??

Diagram 12
Black has good value for the queen!

As often happens once the kings go in different directions, each side then rushes to open lines of attack, and here White has the b-file and Black the g-file, while there is a stand-off on the h1–a8 diagonal! Not surprisingly we may well have reached boiling point...

22...Qxh4!!

With both knights enjoying commanding posts in the centre, the powerful bishop on c6 and the g-file to use, Black is perfectly justified in brutally stripping away his opponent's kingside defences. White has no choice but to go along for the ride.

23 gxh4 Rxg2!

The consistent follow-up that suddenly sees the rest of Black's forces grow dramatically in stature. Note that the rook is immune in the heart of White's position in view of 24 Kxg2 Nf4+ with mate next move.

24 f3

The long diagonal must be closed.

24...Re2! 25 Qd1 Rg8!

Now every piece but the king plays an important role in Black's attack, and White has no time to launch a counter.

26 Bg5

The alternative is to contest the g-file rather than block it: after 26 Rg1 Rxg1+ 27 Kxg1 Black has 27...Rxd2!, while 27 Qxg1 Rxd2 28 Qg8+ Kd7 29 Qf7+ Ne7 sees White outnumbered.

26...h6! 27 Re1

27 Bxh6 Rgg2 is decisive (see the section on the 7th rank in Chapter 4).

27...Rxe1+ 28 Qxe1 Nxf3! 29 Qa5

White finally manages an aggressive move of his own. Instead the attempt to shore up the kingside with 29 Qg3 places the queen on an awkward square, as 29...Nxg5 30 hxg5 Nc3+ 31 Kg1 Ne2+ demonstrates.

29...hxg5 30 h5

Denying Black an open g-file. Hoping for more is futile, as 30 Qxa7 Nc7 defends a8 and threatens to unleash the bishop.

30...a6 31 Rd1 Rh8

Not forgetting the theme that he started, Black switches files in order to renew the onslaught. It is interesting that White's rook is unable to enter the game, while the queen also has nothing to aim at.

 WARNING: The queen can be a lonely piece.

32 Rd3 g4 33 c4 Nc7 (Diagram 12)

Black has twice as many pieces and an armada of pawns, his king is solid and the win is a matter of time.

34 Rd1 Rxh5 35 Kg2 Rxh2+ 36 Kg3

Or 36 Kf1 g3 with the threat of mate on f2.

36...Rh3+ 37 Kf2 f4 38 Ke2 Nd4+! 39 Ke1 Rh1+ 0-1

Game 6
□ **Oll** ■ **Kharlov**
New York 1997

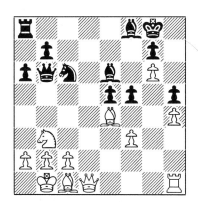

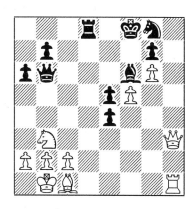

Diagram 13	**Diagram 14**
The g6-pawn is useful	White's attack has borne fruit

Black's pieces point to White's king and the f5-pawn harasses the bishop, but White does have something to smile about in the form of the well advanced g6-pawn, which is close enough to Black's king to entertain ideas involving an offensive. Since material is one of a number of factors we should take into account when evaluating complex situations, our first thought does not necessarily have to be to retreat.

24 f4!

We have already seen how time plays such an important role, so here White's eagerness to strike the first blow leads to the logical opening of the queen's diagonal.

24...fxe4 25 Qxh5 Be7 26 f5! Bd5 27 Qh7+ Kf8 28 Qh8+ Bg8 29 h5

For the piece White has a dangerous attack, and the fact that Black's kingside is now the focus of attention is a sign of the success of White's strategy. Not only is Black's extra piece pinned to the already troubled king, but the marching pawns will soon reduce the other pieces to passive defenders. Whether White has a forced win is another matter – the initiative and the subsequent negative psychological effect on Black is sufficient.

TIP: When the kings are on either side of the board and are vulnerable to attack, a piece sacrifice may well provide the momentum to put your opponent under pressure.

29...Bf6 30 h6 Ne7

Completing the withdrawal of forces. The alternative is 30...Ke7 31 h7, when both 31...Bxb3 32 Qxa8 and 31...Qd8 32 Bg5! are final.

31 h7 Rd8 32 hxg8Q+ Nxg8 33 Qh3 (Diagram 14)

For the moment, at least, the queen has finished work on h8, so the text brings the piece back into the fold, covering the e3-square to activate the bishop. The advantage White earned in attacking mode has been converted to a decisive positional lead, with the e4-pawn a potential target to add to Black's continued worries on the back rank.

33...Qc6 34 Be3 Rd5

Heading for the b-file. If Black looks to the c-file for counterplay with 34...Rc8 White simply drops the queen back to g2, simultaneously protecting c2 and monitoring e4 in readiness of Nc5.

35 Nd2

Note that White's king has not even suffered so much as inconvenience thus far. Black now tries to remedy this.

35...Be7

35...Rb5 36 c4 is excellent for White.

36 Nxe4 Rb5

Black's rook can no longer be hit as in the previous note, the knight is attacked and the queen exerts pressure on the long diagonal. However, using the same no-nonsense logic we encountered when we first joined the game, White once again changes gear.

37 f6!? gxf6

37...Bxf6 38 Nxf6 gxf6 39 Qh8 does not help Black.

38 Bc1!?

Not strictly necessary, perhaps, but this impudent move accentuates the difference between the two sides – Black's king is practically defenceless and White's is safe. Apart from defending b2 the bishop also covers the back rank.

38...Ke8

Obviously 38...Qxe4 needs to be checked: 39 Qc8+ Kg7 40 Rh7+ Kxg6 41 Qxg8+ Kf5 41 Rh5 mate.

39 Qh8 Qe6 40 Rh7 f5 41 Rxe7+

Also good is 41 Rg7 fxe4 42 Rxg8+ Kd7 43 g7!.

41...Kxe7 42 Qg7+ Kd8

42...Ke8 runs into 43 Nd6+! Qxd6 44 Qxg8+ Qf8 (44...Kd7 45 Qh7+ and 46 g7) 45 Qe6+, when White wins after either 45...Qe7 46 Qc8+ Qd8 47 Qxd8+ Kxd8 48 g7 or 45...Kd8 46 Bg5+ Kc7 47 Qf7+.

43 Bg5+ Kc8

43...Ne7 44 Qxe7+! Qxe7 45 g7 and the g-pawn, which started the whole process thanks to its proximity to Black's king, makes the final contribution.

44 Qf7 Qd5

44...Rb6 45 Nc5! Qxg6 46 Qf8+ Kc7 47 Qd8+ Kc6 48 Qd7+ Kxc5 49 Be3+ leads to forced mate.

45 Nc3 Qh1+ 46 Bc1 1-0

It is no coincidence that, with a few exceptions – most notably the instructive use of the bishop – White's play was concentrated almost exclusively on the kingside from the very beginning.

Game 7
□ **Liss** ■ **Leko**
Budapest 1993

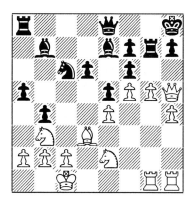 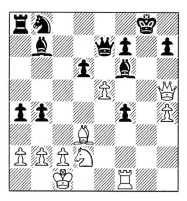

Diagram 15   **Diagram 16**
Attacking with pawn advances   How should White continue?

Now we turn to a more complicated example that requires more vigorous measures in order to trouble the enemy king. On both wings advancing pawns threaten to open up lines of attack, so there is little room, if any, for error.

20...a4?

This is natural but merely pushes the knight to a more useful square, from which c4, e4 and f3 are closely monitored. With his kingside clearly under considerable pressure Black does better to redeploy his knight with 20...Nb8. Then 21 gxf6?! Bxf6 22 Rxg7 Bxg7 23 Rg1 Nd7 is unclear because the knight and bishop work well to hold the kingside. Instead 21 Qh6! Nd7 22 gxf6 Rxg1+ 23 Rxg1 Bxf6 is more awkward for Black, e.g. 24 Ng3 Qf8 25 Qe3 a4 26 Nd2 followed by Nh5 and Nf3-g5 etc.

21 Nd2 Nb8

Surprisingly Black fails to follow up with 21...b3!?, when 22 a3! bxc2 23 Qh6 gives White the better prospects in a messy position.

22 gxf6 Bxf6 23 Rxg7 Bxg7 24 f6!

The beginning of an impressive plan designed to steer a path to Black's king.

24...Bxf6 25 Rf1 Qe7

25...Nd7 26 Bb5! wins for White.

26 Nf4!

The point. White's latest consistent contribution to the cause – note that Black is given no time for his own active operations – threatens to jump into d5.

26...exf4

After 26...Nd7 27 Nd5 Bxd5 28 exd5 Black does not have 28...e4 thanks to the knight on d2. Forced is 28...Nf8, when 29 Ne4 Bg7 30 Rxf7 spells the end.

27 e5 Kg8 (Diagram 16) 28 Rg1+?

Perhaps the most obvious of the two choices, this is certainly inferior to 28 Qxh7+ Kf8 29 exf6 Qxf6 30 Ne4!, e.g. 30...Qe5 31 Qh6+ Ke7 32 Rxf4 Nd7 33 Rxf7+! Kxf7 34 Ng5+ Ke7 35 Qh7+ and wins, or 30...Bxe4 31 Qxe4 Ra7 32 Qxb4 Nd7 33 Rxf4 etc. Given that 33 Rxf7+! is difficult to find, the text is quite natural, as the onus remains on Black to keep his head above water.

28...Kf8!

Not 28...Bg7? when 29 Rxg7+! Kxg7 30 Qxh7+ forces mate.

29 Qh6+ Ke8 30 exf6 Qe3!

Pinning the knight and hitting the rook can't be bad. The potential problem is the queen's location on the e-file.

31 Qg7 Bd5! 32 Kd1 (Diagram 17) 32...b3!!

Perhaps White was expecting 32...Kd8 now that the f7-pawn is protected. Instead the uncompromising advance of the b-pawn suddenly draws our attention to White's king.

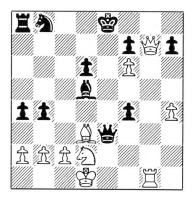

Diagram 17
How can Black get counterplay?

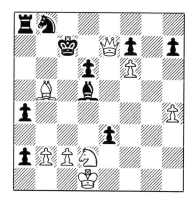

Diagram 18
White must settle for a draw

33 Re1

33 a3!? has been suggested, when 33...bxc2+ 34 Bxc2 Qd4 35 Re1+ Kd7 36 Re7+ Kc6 checks the king to the third rank but is not clear.

33...bxa2

As one queen is about to leave the board another is ready to arrive!

34 Rxe3+ fxe3 35 Bb5+

35 Qg8+ Kd7 36 Bf5+ Kc7 37 Qc8+ Kb6 38 Qd8+ Kc5 again sees the king wander up the board, and this time Black can look forward to a decisive material lead when White runs out of checks.

35...Kd8 36 Qf8+ Kc7 37 Qe7+ Kc8

Black is not interested in 37...Kb6 38 Qxe3+ Kxb5 39 Qa3 etc.

38 Qe8+ Kc7 39 Qe7+ ½-½ (Diagram 18)

An instructive game in which White generated the necessary threats but, at the critical moment, failed to appreciate a counterpunch.

WARNING: With opposite sides castling, always keep an eye on your opponent's marching pawns while conducting your own offensive on the other flank.

Game 8
☐ Leko ■ Kramnik
Belgrade 1995

Despite the potentially vulnerable dark squares White's king enjoys better protection than its counterpart. Add to this White's superior, more aggressive looking forces, and it is clear to whom the advantage belongs.

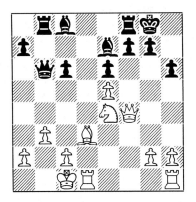

Diagram 19
Whose king is safer?

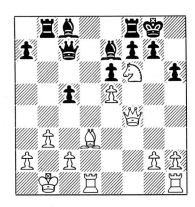

Diagram 20
White opens up the black king

17...Qc7

Already Black must be alert. 17...Ba6, for example, runs into 18 Nf6+!, when 18...gxf6 19 exf6 Ba3+ 20 Kb1 announces mate. Instead after 18...Kh8 19 Qe4 Bxd3 20 Rxd3 White also wins, e.g. 20...g6 21 Rh3 Kg7 22 Rxh6!, or 20...gxf6 21 Qf4 Kh7 22 Rh3.

18 Kb1!

White sensibly avoids the hasty 18 Rhf1 in view of 18...f5! 19 exf6 Qxf4+ 20 Rxf4 gxf6 and the absence of queens drastically alters the situation. Furthermore, with the king now on b1 White need no longer concern himself with any unpleasant checks. Meanwhile Black's kingside structure remains a problem, as we are about to see.

18...c5

Opening the a8-h1 diagonal for the bishop (e4 is a pivotal square for White) and introducing the possibility of pushing to c4. Addressing the problem of the f6-square by occupying it with 18...f6 prompts White to look to the knight's other option: 19 Nd6! fxe5 20 Qe4 Bxd6 21 Qh7+ Kf7 22 Bg6+ Ke7 23 Qxg7+ etc. Also worth consideration is 18...Rd8, when 19 Rhf1 Bf8 20 Nd6! is very good for White in view of the check on h7 should Black take twice on d6. It is no coincidence in these two variations that the d-file plays an important role.

 NOTE: Whoever castles long tends to have more influence on the d-file which, in turn, can facilitate an attack on the kingside.

19 Nf6+! (Diagram 20)

This is just the kind of move we find in 'White to play and win' puzzles, or are not surprised to see when playing through annotated games in books and magazines. However, in a real-life situation we tend to either concentrate on more sober options (Nd6, for example, in this case) or consider and subsequently decline a move such as the text. This is a pity because, in analysing our games later, we have a feeling that this or that sacrifice would have been quite sound.

TIP: When there is little or no sign of your king coming under attack, don't be afraid to exploit the weaknesses in front of your opponent's king on the other flank – even at the cost of material.

In this case the acceptance of the piece opens Black up to a deadly mating attack (see the next note).

19...Kh8

Black calmly tries to ignore the knight – not an easy task! – rather than compromise his pawns. The problem is, of course, that White is allowed to continue to turn the screw while on the other wing there is no sign of a counter.

TIP: Even when no obvious point of entry is available it is reassuring to know that your solid king affords extra time in which to generate play on the opposite flank.

Both captures on f6 must be examined. 19...gxf6? is the first to check and, not surprisingly, after 20 Qxh6 f5 White is able to break the somewhat flimsy defensive shield with the straightforward 21 g4!, e.g. 21...Qxe5 22 gxf5 Bf6 (even here Black manages to threaten immediate mate) 23 Rhg1+ Bg7 24 f6! and the game is over. Perhaps the best try for Black is 19...Bxf6!? 20 Qe4 Rd8 21 Qh7+ Kf8 22 exf6 gxf6, although 23 Bg6! looks unpleasant.

20 Qe4 g6 21 h4!

By now it should be pretty clear that White's general strategy involves the use of rather blunt threats to induce serious structural compromises, making sure that Black is not given sufficient time to drum up queenside counterplay. The latest thrust is guaranteed to make further progress, whether a white or black pawn arrives on h5.

21...Bb7 22 Qf4

Attention now switches to the newly deserted h6-pawn.

22...Kg7 23 Ng4 Rh8!

Accurate defence from Kramnik. Lesser players (i.e. almost anyone else) might hit out on the dark squares with 23...g5? 24 hxg5 Bxg5 but this leads to a forced mate for White thanks to a second piece landing on f6: 25 Qf6+! (remember – material is one of many factors) 25...Bxf6 26 exf6+ Kg8 (26...Kh8 27 Rxh6+ Kg8 28 Rdh1) 27 Nxh6+ Kh8 28 Ng4+ Kg8 29 Bh7+ Kh8 30 Bg6+! Kg8 31 Nh6+ Kh8 32 Nxf7+ Kg8 33

Rh8 mate.

> **NOTE: The more difficult defensive decisions you present your opponent the more likely he is to make a (decisive) mistake.**

24 Rdf1 Rbf8 25 Nf6 Qd8

Not 25...Bxg2? 26 Ne8+! with a fitting finish. Notice how Black is too busy offering support to his king to harbour hopes of mounting an offensive.

26 Qg3 h5

If Black dare venture into enemy territory with 26...Qd4 White has 27 Nh5+ Kg8 (27...Kh7 28 Rxf7+) 28 Bxg6! etc.

27 Qg5

As a student of the positional aspects of attacking play I am impressed by Leko's patient but ruthless treatment of the attack. However, the suggested alternative 27 Nxh5+!? Rxh5 28 Rxf7+ Rxf7 29 Qxg6+ Kf8 30 Qxh5 also looks good, investing a piece to strip away the defences and leave Black's king desperate for shelter. Indeed after 30...Kg8 31 Qg6+ Kf8 32 Qh6+ Kg8 33 Rh3!? White seems to be doing very well.

27...Rh7 28 Rf4 Kh8 29 Rhf1

Thanks to his focused, long-term aggression White has brought all his pieces into the attack.

29...Bxf6 30 Rxf6 Rg8 31 g3!

A cheeky reminder to Black whose pawn structure is superior in case there is a transposition to an ending.

31...Qe7 32 Qf4 Rgg7 (Diagram 21)

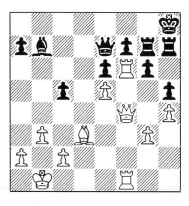

Diagram 21
Black's rooks are rather passive!

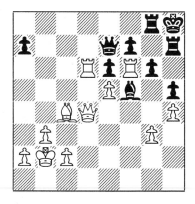

Diagram 22
Black's queenside is now the problem

We need only be aware of how the pieces move to appreciate that White's accumulation of pressure on the kingside has resulted in completely tying up Black's rooks.

TIP: A decent advantage of any kind is the aim when generating an attack against the king – this can be in the form of mate, material gain, superior pawn structure, superior pieces etc.

In Diagram 21 White's obvious advantage allows him to create a new front of attack now that Black's rooks have found the most embarrassing posts available!

33 Rf2 Bd5 34 Kb2 Bc6 35 Bc4 Bb7 36 Rd2!

All change!

36...Rg8 37 Rd6 Qe8?!

37...Qc7 is a lesser evil, but White's domination is sure to lead to something tangible.

38 Qf2! Be4 39 Qxc5 Qe7 40 Qd4 Bf5 (Diagram 22)

Bolstering the kingside and trapping the rook. Unfortunately for Black it is the queenside that now needs help.

41 Rd7 Qe8 42 Qxa7 Rf8 43 a4 Kg8 44 a5 Qc8 45 a6 Qc6 46 Qc7 Qg2 47 Bxe6! Bxe6 48 Rxe6 1-0

Game 9
□ Alvarez ■ Hernandez
Cuba 1996

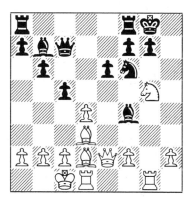

Diagram 23
Which rook should come to d8?

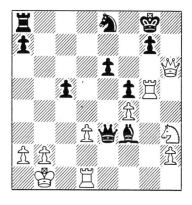

Diagram 24 (variation)
Black is holding the balance

Which rook? This is a conundrum at all levels and, here, with Black to play, the decision is critical. Of course the presence of kings on opposite wings adds to the tension...

18...Rad8?

Perfectly natural, perhaps, but a crucial error. In Yemelin-Epishin, St Petersburg 1996, Black (a strong GM) wisely opted for the other rook. That game continued 18...Rfd8 19 dxc5 bxc5 20 Nh3!? Bxd2+ 21 Qxd2 and now with 21...Ne8! (21...c4? runs into 22 Qc3) Black was able to hold g7, monitor the d-file and plan a later activation of the queen's rook. After 22 Qh6 Qe5 23 Rg5 f5 24 f4 Qe3+ 25 Kb1 Rxd3! 26 cxd3 Bf3 the following position was reached (Diagram 24):

Thanks to the correct rook going to d8 Black has been able to properly defend his king while simultaneously infiltrating White's camp with an exchange sacrifice. With 27 Rdg1 White renewed the assault on g7 but 27...Bg4 28 Nf2 Rb8!! (28...Qxf2? 29 Qxe6+) illustrated the difference between the two available rook moves in the initial diagram position. There followed 29 Qh4 Nf6 30 Qg3 Qd4 31 b3 Nh5 and now White should have returned the exchange on h5 with the better game for Black. Instead 32 Qh4 Nxf4 33 R5xg4 fxg4 34 Qxg4 a5! saw Black finally assume the initiative. Returning to the position after 18...Rad8, redeploying to b8 or c8 will now involve a loss of a tempo, while a closer look at the f8-rook reveals that it does not really contribute to the defence (g7 – not f7 – is the main concern).

19 Nh7!!

A blow that exploits the f8-rook in that it is both a target and a hindrance to the king, which now finds itself without a flight square.

19...Bxd2+

It seems from what follows that the result will be the same whether or not Black inserts this capture, but at least White is the one who must make an important decision here. After 19...Nxh7 20 Bxh7+ Kxh7 21 Qh5+ Black is in trouble after either 21...Kg8 22 Rxg7+! Kxg7 23 Qg4+ Kh7 24 Bxf4 or 21...Bh6 22 Rxg7+! Kxg7 23 Qxh6+ Kg8 24 Rg1+.

20 Qxd2!

NOTE: In opposite sides castling situations in particular there is a fine line between winning and drawing/losing, usually because the attacking side has had to resort to a committal strategy in order to break through, while the very nature of the struggle brings with it the prospect of a quick counter on the other flank.

In this case White's choice of recapture on d2 is as important as which rook came to d8. Indeed, White's desire to keep his queen in reach of the h5-square leads only to a draw: 20 Rxd2? Nxh7 21 Bxh7+ Kxh7 22 Qh5+ Kg8 23 Rxg7+ Kxg7 and White must take perpetual check.

20...Nxh7 21 Bxh7+ Kh8 (Diagram 25)

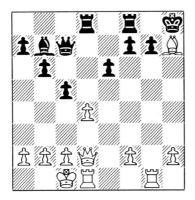
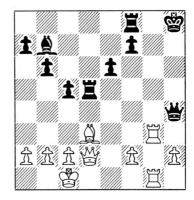

Diagram 25
The extra exchange is meaningless

Diagram 26
The open g- and h-files are decisive

Hoping to slow White down by using the bishop as a shield or threatening to take it later. In view of the continuation 21...Kxh7 22 Rxg7+! Kxg7 23 Qg5+ Kh7 24 Qh5+ Kg7 25 Rg1+ Kf6 26 Qg5 mate this is the best policy.

22 Rxg7!!

The point! It is imperative that such sacrificial possibilities are taken into consideration when evaluating the merits of a brutal attack on the king, especially when there is the constant threat of similar aggression from the opponent on the other wing!

TIP: Include *all* possibilities in your calculations of critical variations – often the key involves a sacrifice.

Taking the second arrival loses immediately, as we see in the next note, so Black must look for other ways to stay in the game.

22...Qe5!?

22...Kxg7 loses to 23 Qg5+ Kh8 (23...Kxh7 transposes to 21...Kxh7, above) 24 Qh6. An obvious counter is 22...Rxd4, when the calm 23 Bd3! simply leaves the rook on g7 (threatening to check on h7). Then 23...Qxh2 24 Rdg1 Rh4 25 Qg5 produces an odd position in which White's three major pieces embarrass the queen and rook on the h-file. Nor does the trade of queens with 23...Qf4 offer Black any respite, as 24 Qxf4 Rxf4 25 Rh7+ Kg8 26 Rg1+ once again highlights the plight of Black's king, trapped by its own hapless rook.

23 Rg5!

After so much hard work it is best to avoid the hoped-for 23 dxe5 Rxd2 24 Rxd2 Kxg7 25 Bd3 Bf3!, when White must restart a new phase of the game. The text, on the other hand, keeps the fire well and truly burning, accentuating the exposed nature of Black's king-side.

23...Qxd4 24 Bd3 Qh4

The fact that the queen has to help the king in this manner is a sign that Black is in trouble.

25 Rdg1 Rd5

25...c4 26 R1g4 Qh3 27 Qc3+ f6 28 Rg8+ leads to mate.

26 R5g3 (Diagram 26) 26...c4 27 Qe3 Rh5

Black, to his credit, has the h-file covered in view of 27...cxd3 28 Rh3.

28 Rg4 Qxh2 29 Qd4+ e5 30 Qd6 1-0

TIP: When considering where to place the rooks in opposite sides castling, try to find a balance between attack and defence.

Eliminating Defenders

This is a simple but neglected tool, the reason being that most players tend to search for ways to increase pressure on a key pawn or square, for example, by finding another piece to attack it. In fact removing the opponent's defender is a better policy because this has the bonus of taking away any other defensive – or, indeed, counterattacking – capabilities this piece may have had.

Game 10
□ Jusupov ■ P.Schlosser
Germany 1997

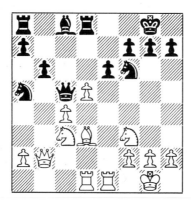

Diagram 27
Black's kingside lacks cover

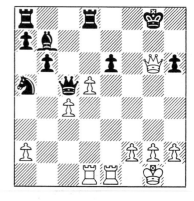

Diagram 28
Black's kingside has been decimated

White's rooks occupy good posts in the centre and both the queen and the bishop point to Black's kingside. Unfortunately for Black the sole defender is the knight and, given that the average Russian professional makes decisions by counting attackers and defenders, Jusupov's next is fairly easy to predict.

17 Ne4! Nxe4

The stubborn 17...Qe7 fails to 18 d6.

18 Bxe4

Simple and best – 18 Rxe4 exd5 19 cxd5 Bf5 is fine for Black.

18...Bb7!

When in doubt, develop/improve a piece. The text connects the rooks, thus strengthening the back rank, and offers much better chances than the rash 18...Nxc4? 19 Qc2 exd5 20 Rxd5! Rxd5 21 Bxd5 and White wins. The more plausible 18...exd5? runs into 19 Qe5!!, when both 19...Nxc4 20 Bxh7+ Kxh7 21 Qh5+ Kg8 22 Ng5 and 19...Bg4 20 Rxd5 Rxd5 21 Bxd5 Bxf3 22 Bxa8 Bxa8 23 Qb8+ Qf8 24 Re8 are final.

19 Ng5!

This time 19 Qe5 (threatening 20 Bxh7+) has less bite after 19...h6, while 19 dxe6? Rxd1 20 exf7+ rebounds on White thanks to 20...Kf8! 21 Rxd1 Bxe4 etc.

19...h6

No doubt part of Black's sensible plan thus far, forcing White to commit if he is to inflict damage on the kingside pawns which, since the trade of knights, are particularly vulnerable. The forcing 19...Nxc4 is exactly that, giving White no choice but to begin working away at Black's defences: 20 Bxh7+ Kf8 21 Qe2!, e.g. 21...Bxd5 22 Qh5 with a menacing initiative, or 21...Rxd5 22 Nxe6+! fxe6 23 Qxe6 with the threat of mate on g8.

20 Bh7+

With this check comes the announcement that White intends to follow the removal of the all-important knight with a further stripping away of Black's protective shield of pawns.

20...Kh8

Black cannot avoid the removal of another defender, even if he goes the other way: 20...Kf8 21 Nxf7! Kxf7 22 Qe5 and Black's king has no friends.

21 Nxf7+ Kxh7 22 Qc2+!

The theme of this chapter is already an indication of what we are aiming to achieve with these attacks, so the latest check gives Black another decision to make regarding his king's survival. Otherwise the automatic 22 Nxd8? Rxd8 23 Rxe6 Nxc4 sees Black fighting back in view of his larger force, White's back rank and the a8-h1 diagonal.

22...Kg8

The alternative is 22...g6, when 23 Rxe6 Rg8 24 Ne5 is one way to keep White in the driving seat.

23 Nxh6+! gxh6 24 Qg6+ (Diagram 28)

Black's once decent looking defences have been completely decimated and there is no way of helping the king.

24...Kf8 25 Qxh6+ Kg8

Or 25...Kf7 26 Qh7+ Kf8 27 dxe6 and mate is inevitable.

26 Qg6+ Kf8 27 Qf6+ Kg8 28 Re5 1-0

Game 11
□ **Z.Almasi** ■ **I.Sokolov**
Wijk aan Zee (open) 1995

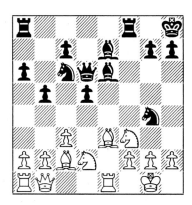

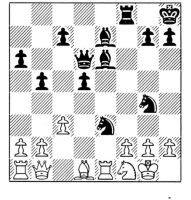

Diagram 29
The h2-square is vulnerable

Diagram 30
How should White recapture?

This time it is Black, to move, who looks the most threatening, with more space, well placed pieces and an advanced knight that teams up with the queen to hit h2. And herein lies the clue to what Black should be trying to achieve – eliminating the defender(s).

17...Rxf3!!

Unlike the previous game there is another knight to replace its partner, but Black has plans for this one, too.

18 Nxf3 Nce5

18...Rf8?, with the intention of sacrificing a second exchange, fails to

19 h3 Rxf3 20 hxg4!, White following the logic that it makes sense to eliminate the attacker! The text has the advantage of both threatening to remove the remaining defender with a like-for-like trade while improving Black's knight, sending it nearer the kingside action.

19 Nd2

White, understandably, is in no mood to part with his only knight. Indeed after 19 Nxe5 Qxe5 White's kingside is in need of help. Hoping for aggressive defence with 20 f4? does not help in view of 20...Qh5 21 h3 Nxe3 22 Rxe3 Bc5 23 Qe1 Bxh3!, while 20 h3 Qh2+ 21 Kf1 Rf8! is very good for Black. This leaves 20 g3 Qh5 21 h4, when the fragile pawns are doomed: 21...Bxh4! 22 gxh4 Qxh4, e.g. 23 Bf5 Qh2+ 24 Kf1 Nxe3+ 25 Rxe3 (25 fxe3 Rf8) 25...Bxf5 26 Qxf5 Qh1+ 27 Ke2 Qxa1, or 23 Kf1 Rf8 24 Ke2 Rxf2+! 25 Bxf2 Qxf2+ 26 Kd1 Ne3+ 27 Rxe3 Bg4+ and mates.

TIP: When a piece that defends against mate can be challenged, this is a sign that some sort of systematic dismantling of the defending king's position might be a possibility.

19...Nc4

The harassment continues, but this time there is the added bonus for Black (if White declines to exchange knights) that White's dark-squared bishop – another key defender – can be taken out of the equation without parting with the g4-knight.

20 Nf1

Foolhardy is 20 Nf3? Rf8 21 h3 Ngxe3 22 fxe3 as Black has the by now predictable 22...Rxf3! with continued – and heightened – pressure.

20...Rf8

Taking up a menacing stance on the f-file, so that points on which to focus are now h2 and f2, with additional emphasis on the related e3-outpost. The immediate 20...Ncxe3 is another possibility.

21 Bd1

With his queen and bishop lined up on the b1–h7 diagonal to provide White with his only threat, dropping back to d1 is not the move White wants to play, but the g4-knight is enormous. With this in mind there is also 21 h3 Ncxe3, when it is a matter of by how much can White limit his opponent's lead. For example 22 fxe3?! Bh4! gives Black a decisive advantage after either 23 hxg4 Bf2+ 24 Kh1 Bxg4 25 Nh2 Rf6! or 23 Re2 Rxf1+! 24 Kxf1 Qh2. Returning the exchange with 22 Rxe3 Nxe3 clearly favours Black, so best is 22 hxg4 Nxg4 when White still has problems, particularly on the dark squares. Finally there is 21 g3 Nge5, the new hole on f3 causing fresh problems.

21...Ncxe3 (Diagram 30) 22 fxe3?

Accurate, albeit uncomfortable for White, is 22 Rxe3 Nxe3. In the diagram position h2 is defended by the knight which, in turn, is in the firing line of Black's rook...

22...Rxf1+!

A purely thematic exchange sacrifice which, like the opener, sees White having to part company with a loyal defender.

23 Kxf1 Qxh2 24 Bf3 Ne5 25 Qd1

The queen finally stirs. The alternative way to lose is 25 Ke2 Nxf3 26 Kxf3 h5, e.g. 27 Rg1 Bg4+ 28 Kf2 Bh4+ 29 Kf1 Qe5! 30 g3 Qf6+ 31 Ke1 Qf3 etc.

25...Bh4 26 Rc1 Bg4! 0-1

Black refused to take his foot off the pedal from the beginning, a series of direct challenges resulting in a final breakthrough.

Game 12
□ **J.Herrera** ■ **Qvesada**
Correspondence 1996

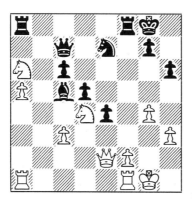

Diagram 31
White's kingside is weak

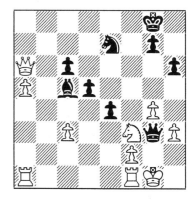

Diagram 32
Black's queen breaks in

Here White's kingside pawns are already weak, and the d4-knight protects the gaping hole on f3. White's queen, too, plays a defensive role. Black's queen, meanwhile, is well placed on c7 (pointing to White's kingside), his king's rook monitors f3 and his knight is ready to jump to action via g6. Imagine White being without the services of both his queen and knight, and it is not difficult to see that the white king would be worryingly exposed...

1...Rxa6!

Effectively eliminating the defender through deflection.

2 Qxa6

Throwing in 2 Ne6 loses immediately: 2...Qg3+ 3 Kh1 Qxh3+ 4 Kg1 Rf3 etc.

2...Rf3!

Exploiting the fact that the bishop stands on the same diagonal as White's king. Note that Black's ambitions are realistic only because the g4-pawn should be home on g2.

 TIP: Advanced pawns in front of a castled king create holes, and these require protection from pieces – look for ways to either remove or deflect these pieces.

3 Nxf3

One of several options, none of which appear to help White. 3 Kg2 seems sensible, when 3...Bxd4 4 cxd4 Ng6 overpowers White, as the following variations demonstrate: 5 Rg1 Nh4+ 6 Kf1 Qh2 7 Ra2 e3; 5 Ra2 Nh4+ 6 Kg1 Rxh3 7 f4 exf3; 5 Rh1 Nf4+ 6 Kf1 Nd3 7 Ra2 Qg3; 5 Qb6 Nh4+ 6 Kg1 Rg3+! etc. Rushing back with 3 Qe2 also meets with 3...Ng6!, when 4 Nxf3 Qg3+ 5 Kh1 Qxh3+ 6 Nh2 Nf4 wins, while 3 Ra2 runs into 3...Rxh3 4 f4 exf3 etc.

3...Qg3+ (Diagram 32)

This is the very move Black needs in order for the strategy to succeed.

4 Kh1 Qxf3+ 5 Kg1

5 Kh2 Bd6+ 6 Kg1 Qxh3 7 f4 Bc5+ 8 Rf2 Qg3+ comes to the same conclusion.

5...Qg3+ 6 Kh1 Qxh3+ 7 Kg1 Qxg4+

This capture is not necessary, and I would be tempted to leave the g-pawn on the board to serve as a reminder to White of his suspect defensive barrier. 7...Bd6 wins.

8 Kh2 Qf4+ 9 Kh1 Qf3+ 10 Kg1 Qg3+ 11 Kh1 Qh3+ 12 Kg1 Bd6 13 f4 Bc5+ 0-1

Stay Alert

The mere mention of the theme 'attacking the king' typically brings to mind scenarios involving pawn storms, sacrifices on h7, g7 or f7 and crushing combinations. However, the safety of the king is an important aspect throughout the game, and we should remember to be alert to the possibility of launching an attack in all circumstances. A common mistake is to not even entertain the existence of such an opportunity, the exchange of queens in a 'normal' position often interpreted as the beginning of a more sober phase of the game.

Here is a good example of how not ruling out very aggressive options in such situations can prove effective.

Game 13
□ **Badea** ■ **J.Pribyl**
Schwabisch Gmund 1995

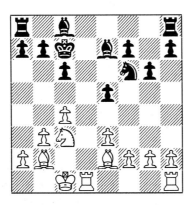
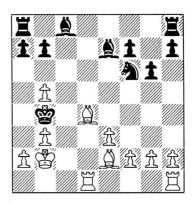

Diagram 33
The queens are off – is Black safe?

Diagram 34
White's king joins the hunt!

The diagram position looks quite sedate, with the queens no longer in play, just the one open file and (already) a drawish symmetry. However, White, to move, is able to exploit the ostensibly safe home of Black's king.

1 Nb5+! cxb5

Or 1...Kb6 2 Bxe5, when 2...cxb5 runs into 3 Bxf6 (3...Bxf6 4 Rd6+).

2 Bxe5+ Kc6

Again 2...Kb6 3 Bxf6 is winning for White.

3 cxb5+!

Forcing the king forward in view of the aforementioned capture on f6. It is already becoming apparent that Black has problems, his king being lured further away from its forces and closer to White's. It is also important that within a couple of moves of the piece sacrifice White has collected two pawns, as this makes it awkward for Black to relieve the pressure with a sacrifice of his own, particularly in view of the fact that we are merely a few trades from an ending.

3...Kc5 4 Bd4+ Kb4 5 Kb2! (Diagram 34)

Adding a sense of irony to the proceedings by giving one king a role in the torment of the other. In fact the text introduces a nasty threat of 6 Bb6! with the intention of following 6...axb6 (preventing 7 a3 mate) with 7 Rd4+ and mate next move.

5...Be6

After 5...Rd8 White changes direction: 6 Bc3+! Kc5 7 b4+ Kb6 8 Rxd8 Bxd8 9 Rc1! and Black loses thanks to the threat of 10 Bd4+.

6 Bc3+

The point of Black's previous move is to meet 6 Bb6 with the spoiler 6...Bc4.

6...Kc5 7 Rc1! Kb6

Black's king is a liability wherever it goes, e.g. 7...Kd6? 8 Rhd1+ etc. Now White can practically wrap up the full point immediately with **8 a4!** due to the unavoidable discovered check once Black's king is forced to the c-file, e.g. **8...Rhc8 9 a5+ Kc7 10 Bxf6+ Kd7 11 Rhd1+** etc. White has two extra pawns and Black will be forced into further passivity preventing the loss of a third.

TIP: The exchange of queens can be as significant a potential loss for the defender as for the attacker – don't stop looking at aggressive possibilities in seemingly calm queenless middlegames.

Finally we turn to an example in which both sides have castled short and both kings are under pressure.

Game 14
□ **Conquest** ■ **Shengelia**
Agios Nikolaos 1997

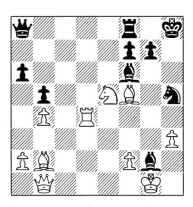

Diagram 35
Both king positions have weaknesses

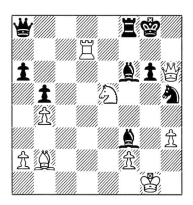

Diagram 36
White has got in

The removal of the g2 and h7 pawns has caused irreparable damage to the respective kings' defensive barriers, and in such a situation it pays to adopt a strategy that revolves around your opponent's key weaknesses. This has the dual purpose of putting him under maximum pressure while distracting him from the exploitation of your own vulnerable king. In this case White, to move, has more pieces pointing at the enemy king, thus affording him the power to create brutal threats.

1 Qd1! g6

Bailing out with 1...Bf3 favours White whether he recaptures with the queen or knight, e.g. 2 Nxf3 Bxd4 3 Bxd4 etc.

2 Bxg6!

If White is to make the most of having the first blow he must play vigorously. It is bad enough for Black that 1...g6 brought his king closer to the now not so distant bishop on b2, but White's latest strips away a second pawn and renews the attack on the stranded knight.

2...Bf3!

When embarking on his assault Conquest had to calculate 2...fxg6 3 Nxg6+ Kg8 4 Qxh5 Bxd4 5 Ne7+ with forced mate.

3 Qd2!

Rather than give himself a chance to drift and Black a chance to find something after 3 Nxf3 White prefers to continue with the forcing theme.

 TIP: Keeping up the momentum of an attack accentuates the opponent's defensive responsibilities while reducing the likelihood of counterplay which, in turn, means the possibility of a serious mistake on your part is considerably reduced.

3...fxg6

After 3...Kg7 4 Bxh5 Bxh5 5 Ng4! all four of White's attacking force contribute to the win.

4 Qh6+ Kg8 5 Rd7! (Diagram 36)

As we will see later (Chapter 4) a rook on the seventh rank is a force to be reckoned with.

5...Bg7

5...Ng7 6 Nxg6 is final.

6 Rxg7+! Nxg7 7 Nxg6! (Diagram 37)

White is a rook down but it is the respective safety of the kings that is the deciding factor. It is interesting that each side is in control of a long diagonal, with White's king ostensibly vulnerable. However, even with the move and the extra rook Black is in trouble because he is defenceless on the dark squares, as we are about to witness. That Conquest had envisaged at the point at which we joined the game is impressive indeed.

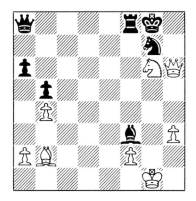

Diagram 37
The extra rook doesn't help Black

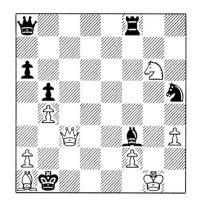

Diagram 38
The king has been driven to its doom

7...Nh5

Let us have a look at the alternatives.

a) 7...Qb7 8 Qh8+ Kf7 9 Qxg7+ is easy.

b) 7...Ne6 8 Qh8+ Kf7 9 Qf6+ and Black is mated.

c) After 7...Nf5 8 Qh8+ Kf7 9 Qf6+ White picks up the rook and knight (or the king).

8 Qh8+ Kf7 9 Qh7+ Ke6 10 Qe7+ Kd5

Or 10...Kf5 11 Nh4+! with mate next move.

11 Qd7+ Ke4 12 Qe6+ Kd3 13 Qe3+ Kc2 14 Qc3+ Kb1

14...Kd1 15 Qd3+ alters nothing.

15 Ba1!! (Diagram 38) 1-0

The king and bishop finally meet. Thanks to Conquest's energetic play Black never had a chance.

Try it Yourself

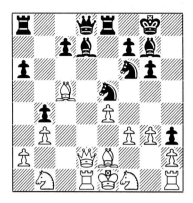

Exercise 1

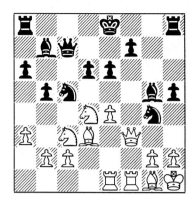

Exercise 2

Exercise 1: How does Black exploit his opponent's poor development?

Exercise 2: Black's kingside efforts have left his king in the centre – a mistake that White is able to punish...

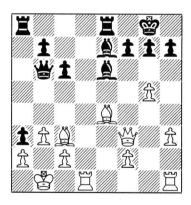

Exercise 3

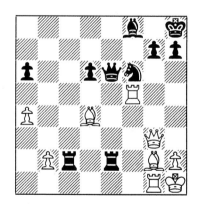

Exercise 4

Exercise 3: The push of White's h-pawn could well meet with the advance of the c6-pawn, so White played 1 Bxh7+? Kxh7 2 Qh5+ Kg8 3 Bxg7 Kxg7 4 Qh6+ Kg8 5 g6. Which of Black's two candidate moves 5...Bf6 and 5...Bg5 is best, and how might play continue in each case?

Exercise 4: How can White, tied down by the unwelcome rooks, strike the first blow?

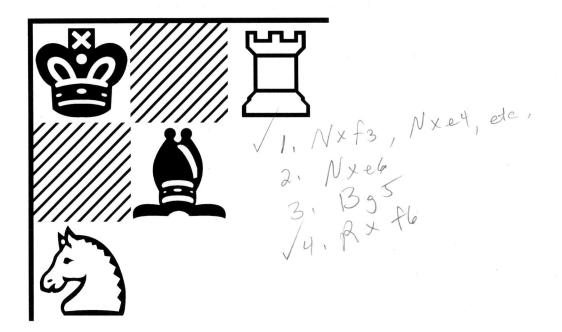

1. Nxf3, Nxe4, etc,
2. Nxe6
3. Bg5
4. Rxf6

Summary

Open lines when the enemy king is in the centre

Look for sacrifices to generate/maintain an initiative

Keep up the momentum

Set your opponent awkward defensive tasks

Try to find a balance between attack and defence

Stay alert!

Chapter Two

Defending – Keep Calm!

- Defence
- Counterattack
- The Knockout Blow
- Nobody's Perfect

There is more to chess than learning theory and studying combinations, pawn structures, endings and so on. We have to sit down at the board and try to reproduce what we know and transfer what we understand about the game under what can be nerve-wracking circumstances, and with time running out! Some players adapt better than others, and it is the ability to stay calm under pressure that ultimately determines our results.

Three of the most tense aspects of a competitive game are defending in a tense situation, counterattacking and finishing off the opponent at the critical moment. There is not a player in the world who has not dropped points in these scenarios! Some players dislike defending so much that they adopt the most aggressive opening repertoire possible in the vain hope that such inconvenience will not befall them. When the inevitable does happen they then crumble.

Unfortunately there is no magic remedy, but it is worth remembering that as material is invested in an attack, and as the situation nears the critical point, the attacker, too, treads the thin line between victory and defeat (or a draw, of course).

Defence

Game 15
□ **Gallagher** ■ **Kobalija**
Biel (open) 1997

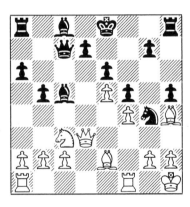

Diagram 1
Black's kingside is a little weak

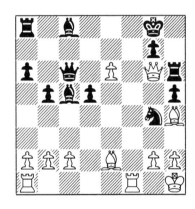

Diagram 2
How does White continue?

White enjoys a development advantage and Black has compromised his kingside slightly. Gallagher, the 2001 British champion, rarely needs much of an invitation to launch an offensive...

15 Nd5!? exd5

Black accepts the challenge.

16 Qxf5 Qc6! 17 e6

Defending along the third rank allows Black to meet the plausible 17 h3 with 17...Qh6! 18 hxg4 hxg4 19 g3 Be7 20 Kg2 d6! 21 Qd3 Bxh4, e.g. 22 Rh1 Qe6 23 exd6 (23 Rxh4 Rxh4 24 gxh4 dxe5 25 fxe5 Qxe5) 23...Bb7!, when Black is still fighting, or 22 gxh4 dxe5 23 Qxd5 Ra7! and Black's king's support, though distant, holds for the time being. The text obstructs the queen and thus steps up the pressure against Black's king.

17...dxe6 18 Qg6+ Kf8 19 f5

In the event of 19 Bxg4? Black has the calm 19...Rh6! before recapturing. This is the kind of move you should be aware of when conducting the defence and, more importantly, such unexpected resources are less likely to feature in the opponent's ambitious calculations.

 TIP: Unexpected defensive resources can throw the attacker off course.

19...Rh6!?

I like Black's mix of aggressive, uncompromising play – even if the ultimate result is to share the point. The very nature of defending means that at some point the attacker has decided to take on such a role and, in doing so, controls the game to some extent. It would be great to emerge from the complications with the full point but, if the attack is reasonably sound, then accurate defence should lead to a draw (i.e. avoiding defeat). 19...Kg8 also seems okay for Black, but is less active and brings with it more opportunity to go wrong, e.g. 20 f6 Ra7? 21 Bxg4 hxg4 22 f7+ Kf8 23 Bf6!! etc. However, 20...Qc7! threatens mate in one and forces White to take a draw after 21 Bxg4 hxg4 22 Qe8+ Bf8 23 fxg7 Qxg7 24 Rxf8+ Qxf8 25 Qg6+ Qg7.

Black's choice in the game both provides the king with a square in the corner and attacks White's queen, thus denying White the luxury of time and, therefore, choice.

20 fxe6+ Kg8 (Diagram 2)

We usually talk of calm, clinical attacking play but here these words can be used to describe Black's reaction to suddenly finding himself on the receiving end of a dangerous attack. In fact the onus is now on White to justify his aggression.

21 Rf8+!

White, too, is holding his nerves well. How many players, with the clock ticking, would play the obvious 21 Qf7+? here? Then 21...Kh8 22 e7 Be6 23 Qf8+ Bg8 spells the end of White's fun and the beginning of misery, since Black is winning. Now the game leads to a draw and, once again, accurate defence is required from Black.

21...Bxf8 22 Qf7+ Kh8

22...Kh7?? 23 Bd3+ leads to mate.

23 Qxf8+ Kh7 24 Bd3+ Rg6!

24...g6? presents White with the choice of taking perpetual check or bringing in more heavy artillery with 25 Re1!?, and I suspect that Joe would take the latter option, and with it good winning chances. Black's cool self-pin, however, is actually the forcing move.

25 Bxg6+

Not 25 e7? Bd7.

25...Kxg6 26 Qf7+ Kh7!

Black is yet to reach the end of the tunnel: 26...Kh6? 27 Qf5! g6 28 Bg5+ Kg7 29 Qf7+ Kh8 30 Re1 keeps the fire burning for White.

27 Qf5+

27 Qxh5+ Nh6.

27...Kg8 28 Qf7+ Kh7 29 Qf5+ Kg8 30 Qf7+ ½-½

Impressive treatment from both players with attack and defence balancing each other out.

TIP: When defending a much harassed king try to find moves that most inconvenience your opponent.

In an ideal world we would all have the tenacious defensive skills of Petrosian and Korchnoi. Unfortunately this is not the case, but that does not mean we should always avoid the capture of ostensibly 'poisoned' or, to a lesser degree, unappetising pawns, for example. At all levels of competition there are opportunities to grab a pawn and subsequently soak up pressure, but such a policy is not to everyone's taste.

The next game is a good illustration of consolidation.

Game 16
□ **Beliavsky** ■ **Akopian**
Pula 1997

I would guess that Black has accepted a sacrificed pawn at some point, resulting in the double attack on his bishop and b-pawn plus the posting of his queen on the same diagonal as White's bishop. Black's plan is simple, of course, namely exchange pieces and win the ending! Alas White will be looking to make the most of his gambit, no doubt with aspirations of a kingside attack.

(Diagram 3) 16...Qe8!

Bringing the queen back to the fold, defending the bishop and indirectly defending the b-pawn with a single move. 16...Qa1? plays into White's hands: 17 Rxd7 Qxc1+ 18 Ne1 Ne5 19 Rxe7 Nd3 20 Kf1 etc.

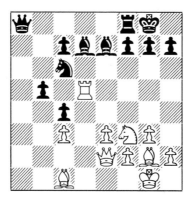

Diagram 3
How can Black coordinate?

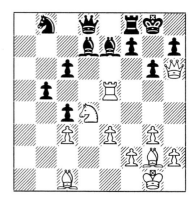

Diagram 4
Black to play – don't panic!

17 Qd1

Obviously not 17 Rxb5? Nd4.

17...Nb8!

Backwards moves tend to be difficult to find but this prepares to consolidate the queenside pawn majority, enabling Black to address the coming kingside offensive.

18 Nd4 c6 19 Re5 Qd8!

The queen has served its purpose on e8, and 19...f6?! 20 Re4 Qf7 21 g4! gives White something to aim at. Furthermore, Black's intended defensive set-up requires that the f8-square is available for the bishop.

20 Qh5 g6 21 Qh6 (Diagram 4) 21...Re8

Black must be careful not to overplay his hand here. For example 21...Bf6? runs into 22 Rh5! gxh5 23 Be4 with forced mate – undoubtedly one of the ideas White has had in mind for a while. Instead, safe in the knowledge that the hefty queenside majority is his trump card, Black appreciates that holding the kingside together is tantamount to a decisive advantage.

22 h4

This time 22 Rh5? gxh5 23 Be4 f5 wins for Black, e.g. 24 Ne6 Bf8! etc.

22...Bf8 23 Rxe8 Bxe8 24 Qf4

White is running out of steam, hence Black's next.

24...c5 25 Nf3 Qd6!

Forcing the exchange of queens in view of the threatened check on d1.

26 Qxd6 Bxd6 27 Nd2 Bc6

Black has a healthy extra pawn and eventually won the game. Unlike the previous example, where Black was simply trying to survive, this time Black's defensive task involved regrouping, consolidating, defending the king and, finally, neutralising the attack to emerge with a modest but ultimately decisive material lead intact.

TIP: Don't sportingly wait to lose!

Game 17
□ **Notkin** ■ **Harlov**
Russian Ch 1994

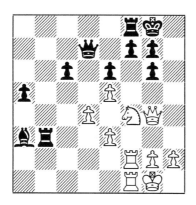 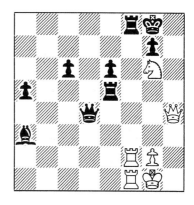

Diagram 5	**Diagram 6**
White must attack	White has good counterplay

We could be forgiven for believing that White, to move, is on the road to a slow but sure defeat, with his e-pawn under fire and the a-pawn free to race down the board. Passive defence is certainly not going to alter the outcome. In fact the only worthwhile alternative to resigning is to throw caution to the wind and generate a distraction in the area in which White has most influence – With all but his d-pawn on the kingside this decision is an easy one...

1 h4!

A good start, unlike 1 Rf3? Rfb8 2 h4 Rxe3! 3 Rxe3 Qxd4.

1...Rxe3

1...Be7 2 h5 g5 3 h6! is sufficiently inconvenient for Black.

2 h5!

Onward. White has to be brutal in his conduct of the attack since concerning himself with who has how many pawns at this stage is futile – the a-pawn is simply too strong. What matters is engineering a situation that affords White some kind of bargaining power.

2...Qxd4 3 hxg6 Rxe5 4 Qh4!

At the critical point of the game White hits upon the key feature of the position. The similar looking 4 Qh3? fails to 4...fxg6 5 Nxg6 Rxf2 6 Qh8+ Kf7 7 Nxe5+ Qxe5 8 Rxf2+ Kg6 9 Qe8+ Kh7, when Black, his a-pawn poised and with three pawns for the exchange, is firmly in charge. The text introduces a crucial difference.

4...fxg6 5 Nxg6 (Diagram 6)

Now there is no time to take on f2.

5...Qxh4 6 Rxf8+ Kh7 7 Nxh4 Bxf8

7...Bc5+ 8 Kh2 Rh5 9 Kg3.

8 Rxf8

Knights are notoriously slow when chasing pawns in the ending, but at least White has a rook to help, ensuring a draw.

8...a4 9 Ra8 Re1+ 10 Kf2 Ra1 11 Nf3 a3! 12 Ng5+ Kg6 13 Nxe6 Kf5! 14 Nd4+ Ke4 15 Nxc6 Kd5 16 Ne7+

Or 16 Nb4+ Kc4 17 Nc2 Ra2 18 Rxa3 Rxc2+.

16...Kc4 17 Nf5 a2 ½-½

TIP: In a 'hopeless' position it is worth trying to generate some kind of counterplay – however futile it might seem – if the alternative is nothing more than passively waiting for a mistake.

Counterattack

Occasionally, when we find ourselves suddenly under attack, the opportunity arises to launch an immediate counter.

Game 18
□ **Franzen** ■ **Baumbach**
Correspondence 1994

(Diagram 7) 24 Be6! Kg7!

24...fxe6 is asking for trouble after 25 Qh6, e.g. 25...Kf7 26 Qh7+.

25 Bxf7! Rh8!

25...Kxf7 26 Qh7+.

26 Qe1 Rxh2+!

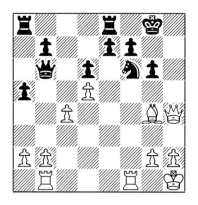 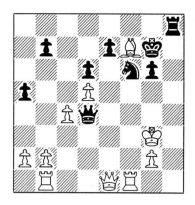

Diagram 7
White is about to launch an attack

Diagram 8
The tables have turned

Turning the tables on White, whose own king is now exposed, albeit at the cost of a rook. Again the bishop is safe in view of 26...Kxf7 27 Qe6+ Ke8 (or 27...Kf8 28 Rxf6+) 28 Rxf6.

27 Kxh2 Rh8+ 28 Kg3 Qd4! (Diagram 8)

Only a few moves ago White began an attack on his opponent's king, yet now he is in danger of losing in embarrassing fashion. Is it time to change course and find a decent defence?

29 Rd1!

In fact the stubborn 29 Qxe7 leads to an amusing draw after 29...Ne4+ 30 Kf3 (30 Kf4? Ng5+! is mate in two, while 30 Kg4? Ng5+! 31 Rf4 Rh4+! 32 Kxh4 Qxf4+ 33 g4 Qh2+! leads to mate on h6) 30...Qd3+ 31 Kf4 g5+ 32 Kf5 Nf6+ (Diagram 9)

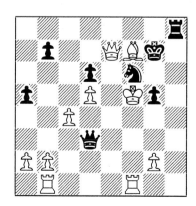 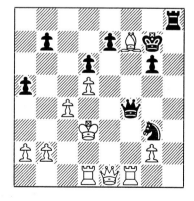

Diagram 9
Who is attacking?

Diagram 10
White activates the king for the endgame!

33 Ke6! (33 Kxg5?? Qg3+) 33...Qe3+ 34 Kxd6 Qb6+ 35 Ke5 Qe3+ etc. The text is preferable because it gives Black chances to slip.

29...Nh5+! 30 Kf3 Qf4+ 31 Ke2 Ng3+ 32 Kd3 (Diagram 10)

White prepares for the ending!

32...Nxf1 33 Qxf1

Perhaps 33 Bxg6!? is playable. Then 33...Rh4!? 34 Be4 Ng3 35 Qc3+ Kg8 36 Bf3 is not clear, but White does have a pawn to compensate for his opponent's active pieces and control of the dark squares.

33...Qxf7

Not 33...Qg3+? 34 Kc2 Rf8 35 Rd3, or 33...Qxf1+? 34 Rxf1 Rf8 35 Kc3 and White's king heads for a4.

34 Qxf7+ Kxf7

The smoke has cleared and the ending is level. The game ended as follows: **35 Rf1+ Ke8!** (35...Kg7? 36 Kc3) **36 Kc3 Rh2 37 Rf2 Rh1 38 Kb3 Rh4!** (38...Rc1? 39 Rc2!) **39 Rc2 b5! 40 a3 bxc4+ 41 Rxc4 Rh5 42 Rd4 Re5 43 Ka4 Re2 44 b3 Re3 45 Rd2 Rc3 46 b4 ½-½**

WARNING: Beware counter-sacrifices.

Game 19
☐ **Aronian** ■ **Sandler**
Yerevan Olympiad 1996

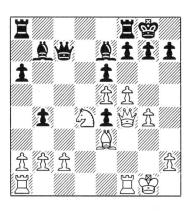

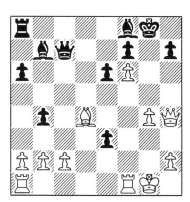

Diagram 11
The pawn advances are double-edged

Diagram 12
Black also has attacking chances

As is often the case in the Sicilian Defence White has pushed the pawns in front of his king in order to storm his opponent's defences. This policy, of course, is not without risk, for if Black is able to open lines for his pieces White's attack is in danger of rebounding. In the diagram position 19 fxe6? fxe6 20 Nxe6 Rxf4 21 Nxc7 Rxg4+ is excellent for Black, so White, having already committed himself, tries an even more direct approach.

19 f6!? gxf6 20 Qh6!?

20 exf6 Qxf4 21 Rxf4 Bc5 favours the bishops. By lodging the queen so close to the target king White puts his opponent under maximum pressure, in turn maximising the defender's chances to falter.

20...Rfd8!

Active defence, bringing the rook to life and vacating f8 for the bishop to evict the queen. Taking on e5 with queen or pawn invites the same response: 20...Qxe5? 21 Rf5!, or 20...fxe5? 21 Rf5!, e.g. 21...exd4 (21...exf5 22 Nxf5; 21...Rfd8 22 Rh5!) 22 Rg5+! Bxg5 23 Qxg5+ Kh8 24 Qf6+ Kg8 25 Bh6 etc.

21 exf6 Bf8 22 Qh4 Rxd4!! 23 Bxd4 e3! (Diagram 12)

One black bishop defends the king while the other has a far more aggressive role in teaming up with the queen to threaten mate. White's attack has come to a standstill, but he does have a 'points' lead.

24 Bxe3 Qxc2 25 Qh3 Rd8 26 Rae1 Qc6! 27 Re2 Rd3 28 Kf2 Bc5! 29 Rfe1 Qe4 30 Kg1

After 30 Kf1 Black can steer the game to an ending with 30...Bxe3 31 Rxe3 Rxe3 32 Rxe3 Qb1+ 33 Re1 Qxb2, when White's more exposed king and weak pawns give Black good winning chances.

30...Bd4

This time 30...Rxe3 31 Rxe3 Bxe3+ 32 Rxe3 Qb1+ is different because White has 33 Qf1 Qxb2 34 Qf2 etc.

31 g5 Qd5 32 Qg3 Be5 33 Qg2

In what are obviously difficult circumstances White finally succumbs to the pressure. 33 Qh3 is dismissed by Sandler in view of 33...Bf4, but 34 Kf2 Qxg5? 35 Rg1 Bxe3+ 36 Qxe3 Qxg1+ 37 Kxg1 Rxe3 38 Rxe3 favours White. Instead Black should turn the screw, e.g. 34...a5 35 b3 Bc6, when White must find a 'passing' move such as 36 Rg1, although 36...Qe5 37 Rge1 Bxg5 looks good for Black since now the h2-pawn is also under fire.

33...Qxg2+ 34 Rxg2 Bxg2 35 Kxg2 Bxb2 36 Kf2 a5 37 Ke2 Rd5 38 h4 a4 39 Rb1 Bc3 40 h5 h6! 41 g6 Rxh5 42 gxf7+ Kxf7 43 Kd3 Rh3 44 Ke4 b3 45 axb3 Rxe3+! 46 Kxe3 a3 0-1

 TIP: Confidence in the availability of general defensive resources creates the confidence required to find counterattacking possibilities.

Game 20
□ **Lobron** ■ **Kramnik**
Dortmund 1995

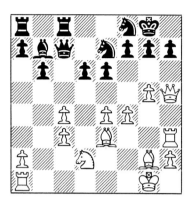

Diagram 13
Black can counterattack

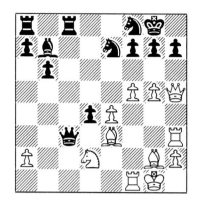

Diagram 14
Black has strong counterplay

The well-known golden rule that action on the flank should be countered in the centre holds true in the diagram position. This time Black has a knight on the back rank to help defend the king, but with White's f-pawn ready to inflict some kind of damage it is imperative that Black waste no time engineering an effective distraction.

20...d5! 21 cxd5

Changing direction with 21 f5 exf5 22 exd5 looks somewhat suspect and invites 22...f4!?.

21...exd5 22 f5

Both 22 Bd4 dxe4 23 Nxe4 Nf5 and 22 e5 Nf5 permit Black to lodge his knight on an excellent square, while (22 e5) 22...d4!? 23 Bxd4 Bxg2 24 Kxg2 Nf5 is an interesting variation on the theme.

22...Qxc3?

22...dxe4! 23 Rf1 (23 f6 g6! and Black's knight comes to f5) 23...Nd5 is more accurate. For example 24 f6?! Nxe3 25 fxg7 Nxf1 favours Black after either 26 Qh6 Qc5+ 27 Kh1 Qf5 28 gxf8Q+ Rxf8 29 Nxf1 e3!? or 26 gxf8Q+ Kxf8 27 Qh6+ Ke8. Best is 24 Nxe4 Nxe3 25 Rxe3 with a balanced game, Black enjoying more freedom here than in the initial position.

23 Rf1?

23 Nb3!? dxe4 24 Bd4 Qc2 25 Rf1!? looks more active. It does seem, however, that White is burning his bridges.

23...d4 (Diagram 14) 24 Bf4

24 f6 Neg6 25 fxg7 works after 25...dxe3? 26 gxf8Q+ Kxf8 27 Rxf7+! Kxf7 28 Qxh7+ Kf8 (28...Qg7 29 Rf3+) 29 Rf3+, but 25...Kxg7 26 Bf4 d3 is far from clear.

24...d3 25 Qh4

25 Kh1!? Qd4 26 Be3 Qd7 27 f6 Neg6 28 fxg7 Kxg7 is complex and Black appears to be holding firm. In fact since he originally broke with the d-pawn Black has seen his position gradually improve, the matter of defending against the kingside assault being more to do with general principles (and decent nerves) than precise calculation.

25...Re8

25...Qd4+!? 26 Be3 Qd7.

26 Qg3 Rad8 27 Rf2?!

Stepping off the g1–a7 diagonal with 27 Kh1 is sensible, when Black should play 27...Qc6!?, switching to the long diagonal and intending 28 Be5 Nxf5!? 29 Rxf5 Qc1+ 30 Nf1 (30 Rf1 Qxd2) 30...d2 etc.

27...Qa1+ 28 Rf1

28 Bf1 Nc6!? with....Nd4 to follow.

28...Qb2

28...Qxa2.

29 Rf2 Qxa2 30 Be5 Nxf5!? 31 exf5 Bxg2 32 Kxg2?

32 g6 fxg6 33 fxg6 Nxg6 is no better but 32 Rxg2 improves, when both 32...Qd5 33 Bc7 (33 Nf3 Rxe5!) 33...Rc8 and 32...Rd5!? are good for Black.

32...Qd5+ 33 Nf3 Rxe5! 34 Qxe5 Qxe5 35 Nxe5 d2 36 Rxd2 Rxd2+

and Black wins. Had Black not blasted open the position White would have been free to patiently conduct his kingside attack, but the introduction of counterplay raised the stakes, upping the tempo to such a degree that White's centre soon deteriorated and his queenside came under fire. Finally the long light-squared diagonal also played an important part in the proceedings, and the long-term hazards of pushing the pawns in front of a castled king while an enemy bishop watches from afar are worth remembering.

The Knockout Blow

The effort required to engineer a decisive advantage is considerable, but the ability to make the win disappear before our eyes when the opponent is on the ropes is a gift we all share! A common occurrence is to arrive at a situation in which one killer theme is set to end the game, the same knockout blow being the winner in more than one instance. The following game is a good illustration of this 'sure thing' scenario.

Game 21
□ **Ljubojevic** ■ **Illescas**
Groningen 1993

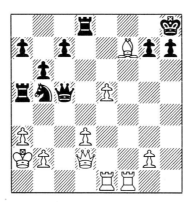 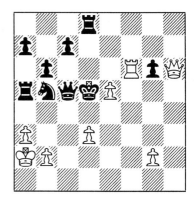

Diagram 15
The bishop is a good long-range piece

Diagram 16
White has run out of steam

Both kings are under pressure and, with three pieces all eyeing the a3-pawn, it seems that Black has the upper hand. However, White's long-range bishop does a good job of both annoying Black's king and covering key squares (a2 and b3) around White's own king. White's queen, too, offers protection. The same cannot be said of Black, whose king is pretty lonely. Hence White's next.

36 Rh1!

With the fairly simple threat of sacrificing on h7 followed by swinging the remaining rook over to deliver mate.

36...g6

Of course 36...Rxa3+ 37 bxa3 Qxa3+ 38 Kb1 Rxd3 had to be considered: 39 Rxh7+! wins. Even in reply to 36...g5, creating an escape route for Black's king, White has ... 37 Rxh7+! Kxh7 38 Rh1+ Kg7 39 Qxg5+ with mate to follow.

37 Rxh7+??

Now the queen comes to h6 with devastating effect, surely?

37...Kxh7 38 Rh1+ Kg7 39 Qh6+

39 e6 cuts the bishop's connection to a2 and b3 and therefore adds decisive punch to 39...Nxa3!. After the text the result is a matter of time...

39...Kxf7 40 Rf1+ Ke6 41 Rf6+

41 Qxg6+ Kd7 42 Qf5+ Kc6 43 Qf6+ Kb7 44 Qxd8 Nxa3

41...Kd5 (Diagram 16)

... Not much time, then, as White has run out of steam!

42 Qd2

On a par with 42 'resigns' but White must have been in shock by now.

42...Nc3+ 0-1

Returning to the position after 36...g6 White has another way to throw away the point: 37 Qh6?? Nc3+ 38 bxc3 (38 Ka1 Rxa3+ 39 bxa3 Qxa3+) 38...Qxa3+ 39 Kb1 Rb5+. However, rather than donate a rook (or king) to Black's cause, White can win with the logical 37 Bxg6! when, to add insult to injury, he is spoilt for choice – 37...Rxa3+ (37...Nxa3 38 Rxh7+ Kg8 39 Rh8+ Kxh8 40 Qh6+) 38 bxa3 Qxa3+ 39 Kb1, or the amusing 38 Kb1!? Nc3+ 39 bxc3 Qb5+ 40 Qb2 Rb3 41 Rxh7+ (that move again!) 41...Kg8 42 Bf7+.

The irony here is the sheer efficacy of Rxh7+ – had this not been such a threat White would have found the winning capture on g6.

Nobody is Perfect

Here is a game to cheer us all up – top players making inexplicable blunders!

Game 22
□ **Ljubojevic** ■ **Anand**
Buenos Aires 1994

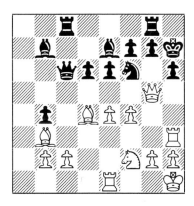

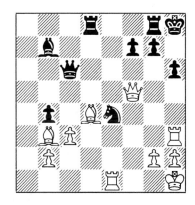

Diagram 17	**Diagram 18**
Black's king is under extreme pressure	Black to play and win

With too many pieces pointing at his king Black is in trouble, especially after White's opener.

23 Ng4 Nxg4

Forced in view of the threatened mate in two.

24 Qxe7!

I promise that this is the only '!' you will see tagged on to a player's move. 24 Qxg4 Qd7 is only clearly better for White, whereas the text is much stronger.

24...e5 25 fxe5 dxe5 26 Bg1 Nf6 27 Qxe5?

The first mistake, missing 27 Bxf7! Rgf8 28 Bg6+! Kh8 29 Rg3 or 29 Qxb4.

27...Nxe4 28 Qf5+ Kh8?

28...Qg6! 29 Qxf7 Qxf7 30 Bxf7 Rgf8 seems to offer Black sufficient compensation for the pawn.

29 Bd4 Rcd8 30 c3?? (Diagram 18) 30...Nd2??

With a bishop and queen lined up against White's king we might be forgiven – particularly after seeing similar examples – for thinking that 30...Nxc3! hits both g2 and the powerful d4-bishop!

31 Qg5?

This time White fails to spot a win on the h1–a8 diagonal: 31 Bd5! wins.

31...Rxd4 32 cxd4 Nxb3 33 d5

At least White remembers that his rook 'defends' his queen so that 33 Rxb3 is out of the question.

33...Re8?

33...Qa6 simply leaves Black with two decent minor pieces for a rook.

34 Rxe8+??

Losing, unlike 34 Qd8!! Then 34...Rxd8 35 dxc6 Bxc6 36 Rxb3 Rd2 37 Rg1 Rd4! is a likely draw.

34...Qxe8 35 Qe3 Qa8

Guaranteeing the win.

36 Rxh6+ gxh6 37 Qxh6+ Kg8 38 Qg5+ Kf8 39 Qh6+ Ke8 0-1

And the moral is: We all make mistakes.

Summary

Look for 'surprise' defensive resources

Inconvenience your opponent

Don't be passive – keep fighting

Have confidence in counterattacking possibilities

Chapter Three

Opening Lines

- Infiltration
- The Diagonal
- Try it Yourself

Since we start the game with an assortment of pieces it makes sense to provide all but the knights (and pawns) with sufficient room for manoeuvre. Our opponents, of course, will be interested only in aiding their own forces and, moreover, will endeavour to restrict our own. The games in this chapter feature examples of infiltrating enemy lines – which tends to use files – and making the most of diagonals.

Infiltration

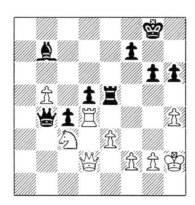
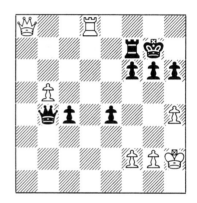

Game 23
☐ **Beliavsky** ■ **Benjamin**
Munich 1994

Diagram 1
White needs a pawn break

Diagram 2
White has broken through

A look at Diagram 1 suggests that we have a stand-off – the passed c-pawn is firmly blockaded, the passed b-pawn is going nowhere and the d-pawn is safe. However, with a simple pawn break White is able to force his way into Black's position.

41 e4!

A thematic thrust that immediately puts White in the driving seat, since the d-pawn is protected by two pieces and attacked four times, while the capture on e4 allows instant access to the back rank.

41...dxe4 42 Rd7! Re7 43 Rd8+ Kg7 44 Qd4+ f6

Also possible is 45 Rb8, but the direct text helps White accentuate his influence on the eighth rank.

45 Nd5! Bxd5 46 Qxd5 Rf7 47 Qa8! (Diagram 2)

Thanks to the challenge in the centre White has been able to transform the game, bullying his way through what seemed like a sound defensive wall. Whether this is enough to win the game is another matter, since the initial position offered little in the way of winning prospects, whereas now the onus is on Black to make the correct decisions.

47...h5?!

47...f5 48 Rg8+ Kf6 49 Qc6+ Ke5 50 Rd8 is decisive, but perhaps Black should try his luck with 48...Kh7 49 Rh8+ Kg7 50 Qg8+ Kf6 51 Rxh6 Rg7, e.g. 52 Qd5 c3.

48 Rg8+ Kh6 49 Qxe4 f5

After 49...Rg7 50 Rh8+ Rh7 51 Qf4+! Kg7 52 Rb8 the party is over, e.g. 52...Qe7 53 Rc8 etc.

50 Qe6

White is winning.

50...Rg7 51 Rh8+ Rh7 52 Qe3+ Kg7 53 Qd4+ Kh6 54 b6 1-0

Black resigned in view of the coming 55 Qf4+ Kg7 56 Rxh7+ Kxh7 57 Qc7+ Kh6 58 b7. As I mentioned earlier, the improved practical chances afforded to White after the infiltration are what matters (see the section on Altered Circumstances in Chapter 6).

TIP: A well timed break directed against a fixed pawn can result in an effective infiltration.

Game 24
☐ **Miezis** ■ **Atalik**
New York 1998

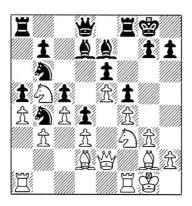

Diagram 3
Black finds an interesting plan

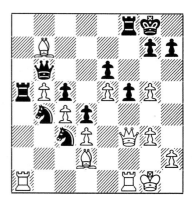

Diagram 4
Black has useful outposts

Here we have a deceptively tense situation arising from a traditional variation of the King's Indian Attack. The very closed nature of the position means that any capture might prove committal and allow the opponent to get the better of resultant open lines. Nevertheless, Black, to move, decided to change the pace of the struggle.

16...Bxb5!?

16...Bc6 is enough for equality, but Black has seen an interesting possibility.

17 axb5

17 cxb5 hands relinquishes control of the important d5-square.

17...a4 18 bxa4 Nxa4 19 Ng5

Inviting Black to enter a bishops versus knights scenario. 19 Rfc1 has been suggested as an improvement, when 19...Nc3?! 20 Bxc3 dxc3 21 Rxa8 Qxa8 22 Rxc3 Qa1+ 23 Qe1 Qb2 24 Qc1 Qxc1+ 25 Rxc1 Nxd3 26 Ra1 sees the wrong player – from Black's point of view since he instigated the process – take control of the a-file. Instead 19...Qd7 20 Qd1 Nc3 improves for Black, e.g. 21 Bxc3 dxc3 22 Rxc3 Rxa1 23 Qxa1 Nxd3, or 22 Rxa8 Rxa8 23 Rxc3 Ra2, when Black has succeeded in injecting some activity into his position.

19...Bxg5 20 Bxb7 Ra5 21 fxg5 Nc3 22 Qf3 Qb6 (Diagram 4)

Black has achieved his aim of infiltrating the queenside in order to unbalance the position. For the invested pawn Black has good outposts for his pieces and the makings of an invasion down the board's only open file.

TIP: In 'lifeless' situations investigate possibilities that lead to a less clear position in which you have one or more open lines and advanced outposts.

23 g4?

White unjustifiably seeks to unsettle his opponent over on the kingside. A better way of doing this might be to return the pawn with 23 g6 hxg6 24 Bg5, although 24...Rb8 25 Bc6 Rxa1 26 Rxa1 Qc7 27 Kg2 Nxc6 28 Qxc6 Qxe5 seems to favour Black.

23...Rxa1 24 Rxa1 fxg4 25 Qg2 Nxd3!

Perhaps White had considered only 25...Qc7 26 Be4! here, but the positive text sees the knights stand side by side within striking distance of the kingside.

26 Qc6

The point behind Black's previous move is that 26 Ra6 now loses to 26...Qxb7! 27 Qxb7 Ne2+, e.g. 28 Kg2 Rf2+ 29 Kh1 Rf1+ with mate next move.

26...Qa5!! (Diagram 5)

After Black's brave endeavours to open the position this excellent move deserves to win! Note that White's impatient attempt to demonstrate a similar desire on the kingside has served only to provide Black with another open file.

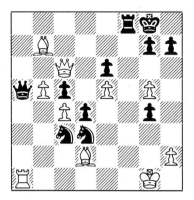

Diagram 5
A brilliant sacrifice

Diagram 6
White's pieces are far away

27 Qxe6+

The most stubborn defence is 27 Rf1!, when Black continues 27...Ne2+ 28 Kg2 Nef4+! (28...Ndf4+? 29 Rxf4 Nxf4+ 30 Bxf4) 29 Bxf4 Nxf4+ 30 Kh1 Qd2, e.g. 31 Qe4 (31 Qxc5 Qe2) 31...Nh3 32 Rxf8+ Kxf8 33 Qb1 d3 34 Qf1+ Qf2 etc.

27...Kh8 28 Bxc3

This time 28 Rf1 sees the game end 28...Ne2+ 29 Kg2 Nef4+ 30 Bxf4 Nxf4+ 31 Rxf4 Qd2+, while 28 Rd1 loses to 28...Ne2+ 29 Kg2 Qxd2! (30 Rxd2 Rf2+ mates).

28...Qxc3 29 Qa6 (Diagram 6)

Or 29 Rd1 Ne1.

29...Nc1 0-1

As we have seen when the kings reside on opposite flanks, the most effective plan tends to involve attacking your opponent's king! In our latest example White, to move, can exploit Black's advanced queenside pawns to seek an opening of lines and subsequent infiltration directed at the black king.

Game 25
□ **Lautier** ■ **Gelfand**
Amsterdam 1996

(Diagram 7) 19 a4!

Almost an automatic choice given that the rook already occupies the a-file. Black needs to hold the defensive lines the best he can, and his next is more or less forced.

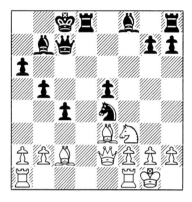

Diagram 7
White wants to break Black's pawn cover

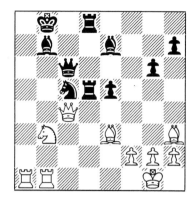

Diagram 8
Mission accomplished

19...Nc5 20 axb5 axb5 21 b3!

Again, once we are acquainted with the theme it seems easy to fall on this move, which further undermines the fragile pawn chain that was shielding Black's king. Just one of the three queenside files would be enough to offer White something in terms of probing enemy lines, but the text aims to gain access to more entry points.

21...cxb3

21...Bd6 denies White's queen access to b5. Then 22 Bf5+! Kb8 23 bxc4 Rhf8 24 Bh3!? does actually shore up the kingside for White as after 24...Bxf3 25 gxf3 Black will miss his bishop (Rfb1 is coming). This leaves 24...e4 25 Nd4 Bxh2+ 26 Kh1, when Black's days are numbered.

22 Bf5+ Kb8 23 Qxb5 g6

Putting the question to the bishop before defending along the fourth rank. The immediate 23...Rd5 leads to at least a clear advantage to White after 24 Bxc5! Bxc5 (24...Rxc5? 25 Qe8+ Bc8 26 Be4! is worth remembering) 25 Qxb3, when we see that White's chipping away at the queenside pawns has culminated in opening all the relevant files!

24 Bh3

Covering g2, just in case.

24...Rd5 25 Rfb1!

Threatening simply to round up the b3-pawn after Nd2. This time 25 Bxc5 Bxc5 26 Qxb3 allows Black unnecessary counterplay with

26...e4.

25...Qc6 26 Qc4 Be7 27 Nd2 Rhd8 28 Nxb3 (Diagram 8)

Mission accomplished.

28...Qa4

No better is 28...Nxb3 29 Ba7+ Kc7 30 Qxb3, e.g. 30...Bc5 31 Rc1! or 30...Rd3 31 Qf7 etc.

29 Nxc5!

Note that White's bishop both defends g2 and covers the flight square on c8.

29...Rd1+ 30 Rxd1 Rxd1+

30...Qxc4 31 Rxd8+ Bxd8 32 Nd7+ Kc7 33 Rc1.

31 Rxd1 Qxc4 32 Nd7+ 1-0

White wins back the queen with interest.

 WARNING: Pawn chains tend to make poor defensive walls when a break is possible.

Game 26
□ **Psakhis** ■ **V.Milov**
Israel 1998

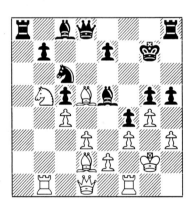

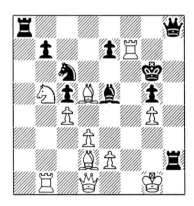

Diagram 9	**Diagram 10**
Black's rooks are dangerously poised	A calm response is needed

In Game 24 White was confused by his opponent's queenside initiative only to see Black's forces ultimately find a way into his kingside. Here Black, to move, already has the a-file and can consider coming to the seventh rank at some point, but his other rook stands menacingly on the h-file...

21...hxg4 22 hxg4 Bxg4!

Milov prefers this to 22...Rh4 23 Rh1 Qh8 24 Qe1 Ra2 25 Rd1, which he evaluates as unclear. Of course the text involves a piece sacrifice, but the prospect of an invasion is no less significant.

23 fxg4 f3+ 24 Rxf3!

Accurate, active defence in a 50–50 situation. The alternative is too passive: 24 Bxf3 Rh2+ 25 Kg1 Qh8 26 Bxg5 (26 Rf2 Bg3! 27 Bc3+ e5 28 Bg2 Rf8! 29 Rxf8 Rh1+! 30 Bxh1 Qh2+ is an instructive variation) 26...Qh3 and Black wins, e.g. 27 Rf2 Qg3+ 28 Rg2 Rxg2+ 29 Bxg2 Rf8, or 27 Qe1 Nd4! 28 Nxd4 Rh1+! 29 Kf2 Bxd4+ 30 e3 Ra2+ 31 Qe2 Rh2+ 32 Ke1 Bc3+ 33 Kd1 Qxf1+ 34 Qxf1 Rhd2+ 35 Ke1 Rdb2+ etc. By taking with the rook White keeps in touch with the f7-square, thus reminding Black that his own king is susceptible to attack.

NOTE: Open lines are important to defenders as well as attackers!

24...Rh2+ 25 Kg1 Qh8 26 Rf7+

26 Re3 Rh1+! 27 Bxh1 Qh2+ 28 Kf1 Qxh1+ 29 Kf2 Rf8+ 30 Rf3 Qh2+ 31 Kf1 Bg3 32 Bc3+ Nd4 33 Bxd4+ cxd4 and the more obvious 26 Rf2 Rxf2 27 Kxf2 Qh2+ win for Black.

26...Kg6 (Diagram 10) 27 e3!!

Calm play indeed. Having seen Black engineer a situation in which he has two major pieces on a file neighbouring White's king, White wastes no time threatening to do exactly the same! In fact the onus is now on Black, who has invested a piece in the attack, to accurately follow up the infiltration.

27...Qh3?!

After 27...Rh3 28 Rf2 Rg3+ 29 Bg2 and 28...Rf8 29 Rxf8 Qxf8 30 Qe2 Rg3+ 31 Bg2 White emerges with his kingside and material lead intact, while 27...Ra2 28 Qf3 Raxd2 29 Be4+ Kh6 30 Qf5 turns the tables completely. Black's best is 27...Rh1+! 28 Bxh1 Qh2+ 29 Kf1 Qxh1+ 30 Ke2 Qg2+ 31 Rf2 Qxg4+, or 30...Qxd1+ 31 Kxd1 Kxf7 32 Nc3 Bxc3 33 Bxc3 Ra3, with a level game in both cases.

28 Qf3 Qxf3 29 Rxf3 Rxd2 30 Rbf1 Bf6 31 Nc7?!

Missing 31 Be4+! with a clear advantage to White, e.g. 31...Kf7 32 Nd6+! Kg7 (32...Kf8 33 Rf5) 33 Nf5+ Kf8 34 Nxe7 Kxe7 35 Rxf6 Ne5 36 Rb6, or 31...Kg7 32 Nc7. Now, with correct play, Black can draw.

31...Rh8

31...Raa2 is tempting but favours White after 32 Be4+ Kf7 33 Rf5. Instead Black relies on the h-file once more.

32 Be4+ Kf7 33 Nd5 Rh6?

33...Ne5! is sufficient to draw: 34 R3f2 Rxf2 35 Kxf2 Nxg4+ 36 Kg3

Ne5 37 Rb1 etc.

34 Rf5?

Returning the favour. 34 Nxf6! Rxf6 (34...exf6 35 Rf5) 35 Rf5 is difficult for Black.

34...Rh3! 35 Nxf6 ½-½

I believe 35...Rg3+ 36 Kh1 Rh3+ is a fitting draw.

The Diagonal

Game 27
☐ **Z.Almasi** ■ **Khalifman**
Ubeda 1997

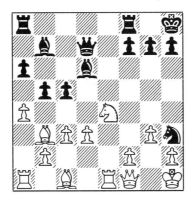

Diagram 11
The long diagonal is useful for Black

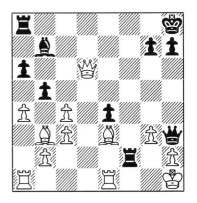

Diagram 12
Exploiting the diagonal

Here we have a typical position from the Marshall Gambit of the Ruy Lopez, a key feature being the h1–a8 diagonal, upon which stand White's troubled king and pinned knight. Black, to move, can seek to undermine the pin immediately with the direct 21...Nxf2+! 22 Qxf2 f5 23 Qg2 (23 Qe2 c4! 24 dxc4 Bxe4+ 25 Kg1 Bb7!?) 23...c4! 24 Bc2 cxd3 25 Bxd3 fxe4 26 Bxe4 Rae8 27 Bd2 Rxe4! 28 Rxe4 Bc5 29 Bf4 Qd3 30 Rae1 bxa4 and Black is slightly better. Instead Black's choice in the game is equally thematic.

21...c4 22 dxc4?!

Given that Black's strategy is pretty clear – exploiting the long diagonal – it seems too accommodating to take on c4. More sensible is 22 Bd1! with the idea of bolstering the position by transferring the bishop to f3. For example 22...cxd3 23 Bf3 Qf5 24 Kg2 sees White's kingside adopt an air of respectability. Again Black has 22...Nxf2+ 23

Qxf2 f5, but now 24 Bf3 fxe4 25 dxe4 Rae8 is level.

22...Nxf2+ 23 Qxf2 f5 24 Qd4?!

24 cxb5? fxe4 25 Qe3 Rf3 26 Qd4 e3 illustrates the power of play on diagonals, while 24 Bf4 fxe4 25 Qe3 Rxf4! 26 gxf4 Bxf4 27 Rad1 (27 Qxf4? e3+ 28 Kg1 Qc6) 27...Qxd1 28 Bxd1 Bxe3 29 Rxe3 bxc4 clearly favours Black. However, with 24 Be3! Qe6 25 Bc2 fxe4 26 Qe2 bxc4 White is able to limit his opponent to an edge.

24...fxe4 25 Be3 Qh3!

Homing in on White's king, the influence of the light-squared bishop allowing Black to part with its partner. Nonetheless this bishop also plays an important role, for example 26 Kg1 Bxg3! 27 Re2 Rf3 28 Rg2 Rxe3!, or 26 Qd2 Bxg3 27 Qg2 Qxg2+ 28 Kxg2 Bxe1 29 Rxe1 bxc4 30 Bxc4 Rac8 31 b3 Rc6! etc.

26 Qxd6 Rf2! (Diagram 12)

TIP: When your opponent's king resides on the same 'closed' diagonal as your bishop, look for ways to clear a path, usually through a sacrifice/deflection.

27 Bxf2 e3+ 28 Qd5 Bxd5+ 29 cxd5 exf2 30 Rf1 Rf8

The f-pawn is strong and White's kingside remains weak.

31 axb5 Qg4

31...h5 also looks good.

32 Kg2 Qf3+

Not 32...Qe4+ 33 Kh3 Rf6? 34 Rxa6.

33 Kh3 Rf5 34 Ra4 Rh5+ 35 Rh4 Rxh4+ 36 Kxh4 Qe2 0-1

Game 28
□ **Akesson** ■ **Speelman**
Pula 1997

Black, to move, has pieces on two diagonals. A natural move, such as bringing a second rook to the d-file, for example, would merely invite White to plant his pawn on e4, cementing the d5-pawn and effectively closing out Black's queen and bishop simultaneously. Consequently Black is practically steered to the appropriate continuation through sheer necessity – not that Speelman needs any clues!

20...e4! (Diagram 13)

Beating White to the punch, opening one long diagonal for the bishop while reminding White that the other could now be a problem.

21 fxe4 Re8 22 Qc2 f5!

Thematic. The key to Black's opener is to clear lines and earn freedom for his pieces, a much better prospect than allowing the fixed structure mentioned in the first note.

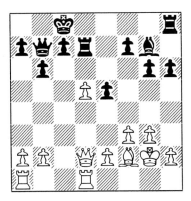

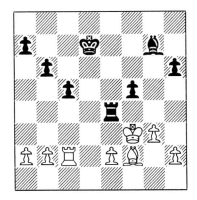

Diagram 13
Black must prevent White's e2-e4

Diagram 14
The endgame is about level

TIP: Always strive to offer your forces maximum potential, even at the cost of a pawn if the alternative is passivity.

23 exf5

White's hopes of erecting a pawn chain on the h1–a8 diagonal disappeared when a black pawn arrived on e4, so he might as well keep taking pawns. Otherwise Black should emerge on top, e.g. 23 Rac1 Rxe4 and after both kings are taken off a hazardous diagonal and file respectively, with 24 Kg1 Kb8!, play might continue 25 b3 Re5 26 Bd4 Rexd5 27 Bxg7 Rxg7! (not 27...Rxd1+?? 28 Rxd1 Rxg7 29 Rd8+), or 25 Rd3 Re5 26 d6 Rxd6 27 Rxd6 (27 Bd4 Rxe2 28 Qxe2 Bxd4+ 29 Rxd4 Rxd4) 27...cxd6 (intending to meet 28 Bd4? with 28...Rxe2!), with an extra pawn for Black in both cases.

23...Rxd5 24 Kg1 gxf5

Black plans to use the e4-square in the coming ending. 24...Rxf5 gives the game a more complex character, e.g. 25 Rac1 Re7 26 Qd3! Rf8 27 Qxg6 Bxb2 28 Qxh6 Rh8 29 Qg5 (29 Qd6 Reh7) 29...Qe4 30 Rc4 Qxc4 31 Qxe7 Qxa2 with an interesting race in prospect.

After **25 Rac1 Rxd1+ 26 Rxd1 Qe4 27 Rd2! Qxc2 28 Rxc2 Re4 29 Kg2 c5 30 Kf3 Kd7 (Diagram 14)** Speelman went on to convert what is currently a roughly level ending (as he has done many times). By making use of the h1–a8 diagonal on his own terms – and denying White the privilege – Black put his opponent under unexpected pressure to handle the ending.

TIP: The process of concentrating on a diagonal does not have to be exclusively linked to attack.

Game 29
□ An.C.Hernandez ■ Moreno Ramon
Cuba 1994

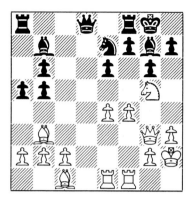

Diagram 15
White has a fine attacking position

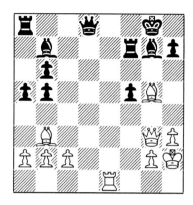

Diagram 16
White's pin is overwhelming

White's forces are primed for attack, and his next move immediately asks difficult questions of Black.

1 f5!

Clearing the way for the hitherto dormant dark-squared bishop and prising open Black's defence in order to increase the scope of its partner on the a2-g8 diagonal.

1...exf5

1...h6? deservedly runs into 2 Nxf7!, e.g. 2...Rxf7 (or 2...Kxf7 3 Bxe6+ Ke8 4 e5) 3 Bxe6 gxf5 4 Bxh6. White ignores 1...a4 and pushes: 2 f6 Bxf6 (2...axb3 3 fxg7 Kxg7 4 Rxf7+) 3 Rxf6 axb3 4 axb3 followed by Ref1.

2 exf5 Nxf5 3 Rxf5! gxf5 4 Nxf7! Rxf7

For the moment White has parted with a rook for the cause, the result being debilitating pins on the a2-g8 diagonal and the g-file.

TIP: A pin on a diagonal – particularly one that exerts pressure on the enemy king – can be more effective than winning material.

5 Bg5! (Diagram 16)

A pinned piece has no power, so the text threatens to invade on e7. 5 Bh6? might look good but after 5...Kh8! 6 Bxf7 Bxh6 7 Re8+ Qxe8 8 Bxe8 Rxe8 White's queen is outnumbered.

5...Qd4

5...Qb8 6 Bxf7+! Kxf7 7 Re7+ Kf8 8 Rc7! spells trouble for Black.

6 c3 f4

In the game White played 7 Bxf4? and soon won after inaccurate play from his opponent. However, **7 Bxf7+! Kxf7 8 Re7+ Kg8 9 Bxf4 Qf6 10 Rxb7** is a simple route to a near decisive advantage.

Game 30
☐ **Lozakov** ◼ **Barbulescu**
Bucharest 1993

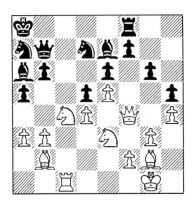

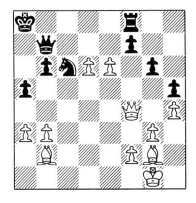

Diagram 17	**Diagram 18 (variation)**
Can White open the long diagonal?	Black is shredded on the diagonals

No prizes for guessing with which diagonal we are concerned here! Quite simply the d5-pawn is in the way and, with *both* the king and queen sharing the long diagonal with the bishop, it is worth taking time to check if it is possible to blast a way through.

1 Nxd5! exd5 2 Ne3!

One down, one to go.

2...Bb5

2...Rc8 3 Rxc8+ Qxc8 4 Nxd5.

3 Nxd5 Bc6 4 Rxc6!

Control of the long diagonal is paramount since the rewards are considerable.

4...Nxc6 5 Nxe7 Ndxe5

At first it seems that Black might be able to hold out with 5...Ndb8 6 Nxc6 Nxc6 7 d5 Nd8 8 d6 Nc6, but White then has 9 e6 (Diagram 18).

As in the previous example, the pin can be traded in for points.

6 dxe5 Qxe7 7 Bxc6+ Ka7 8 Bf3 Qe6 9 Qe4

White has amply demonstrated the power of the diagonal!

9...Rb8 10 Qd5 1-0

Game 31
□ **Lagunov** ■ **B.Schneider**
Berlin 1994

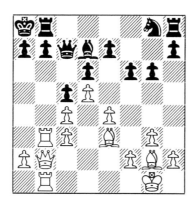

Diagram 19
White's major pieces need help

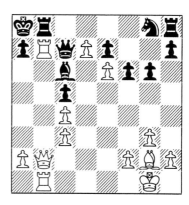

Diagram 20 (variation)
White has blown the position open

The combined power of three major pieces on a single file is obvious, but here White's major pieces need assistance if there is to be a breakthrough.

1 Bxc5!! dxc5

Taking with the queen abandons the b7-pawn, while after 1...b6 2 Be3 White threatens to progress by pushing the c-pawn, 2...Qxc4 losing to 3 Bxb6! axb6 4 Rxb6 etc.

2 e5 Bc8

Or 2...Qc8 3 e6! with two possible continuations.

a) 3...Ba4 4 Rxb7! Qxb7 (4...Rxb7 5 d6 Bc6 6 d7) 5 Qxb7+ (not 5 d6?? Qxg2+ 6 Kxg2 Rxb2) 5...Rxb7 6 d6 and Black has an extra rook and knight yet, thanks mainly to the g2-bishop, is completely lost.

b) 3...Be8 4 d6 Bc6 5 d7 Qc7 6 Rxb7! (Diagram 20)

Mate is imminent: 6...Rxb7 7 Qxb7+ Bxb7 8 Bxb7+ etc.

3 d6 exd6

3...Qd7 4 e6! and Black cannot hang on to b7.

4 Qa3! 1-0

White still has a chance to go wrong here with 4 exd6? Qd7 5 Qa3 Qxd6 when Black's queen has access to a6. With 4 Qa3!, however, White threatens 5 Qxa7+! Kxa7 6 Ra3+ etc. (4...a5 loses to 5 Rb6).

Game 32
□ **Tiviakov** ■ **Sherbakov**
Russia Ch 1994

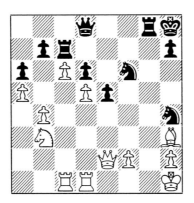 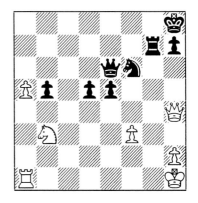

Diagram 21
Can Black get at the white king?

Diagram 22
Both kings are vulnerable

White has a decent passed pawn in the making on c6, well placed rooks and considerable influence on the light squares. What can Black do to avoid slipping into a poor position?

33...Qa8!!

Hopefully the examples in this book should inspire us to find such imaginative moves in our games! The a8-h1 diagonal is, in fact, a potential problem for White, whose king position looks all the more precarious with Black's rook keeping guard on the g-file.

34 Be6

34 f4!? bxc6!? 35 fxe5 cxd5! 36 Nd4 Rxc1 37 Rxc1 Ne4 38 exd6 Qf8 39 Rf1 Qxd6 is unclear.

34...Re8! 35 Qe3 bxc6!

It is not clear which of these strong GMs has seen further here, but Black's idea is anyway very nice.

36 Qg5 Rxe6!

It is interesting that once a player has hit upon a specific – and far from obvious – theme during a game, related ideas tend to spring to mind. In this case Black's appreciation of the significance of the a8-h1 diagonal seems to present him with opportunities based on the theme.

The point of the text, for example, is that 37 dxe6?? loses to 37...c5+ — this might be easy to spot at this stage, but much less so before the queen arrived on the unlikely a8-square!

37 Qxh4 Rg7!

Clinical play. A mistake is 37...Nxd5? in view of 38 Rxd5!, e.g. 38...Rg7 39 Rd3 c5+ 40 f3 e4 41 Re3, or 38...cxd5 39 Rxc7 d4+ 40 Kg1 Rg6+ 41 Kf1 Qh1+ 42 Ke2 d3+ 43 Kd2.

38 dxc6!

38 Rxc6? Nxd5! clears the diagonal in Black's favour.

38...d5 39 b5!? axb5 40 f3 Rxc6 41 Rxc6 Qxc6 42 Rc1 Qe6 43 Ra1 (Diagram 22)

The transformation has resulted in Black having a modest material lead and White a supported passed pawn. Meanwhile both kings are susceptible to attack, a feature of the position to which Black now turns.

43...Ne4!?

Designed to exploit White's cornered king and, ultimately, the long diagonal once again. 43...d4 is Sherbakov's proposal, e.g. 44 a6 Qc6! 45 Nd2 Qc3 46 Qe1 Ra7 47 Rc1 Qe3.

44 fxe4

44 Rg1?? Qf6! and 44 Rc1 Qh3!! help demonstrate the plight of White's king.

44...Qg6 45 Qd8+ Rg8 46 Qxg8+ Qxg8

Not 46...Kxg8?? 47 Rg1.

47 a6 dxe4 48 a7 Qa8

Again. This time, however, Black's queen combines defence with a long-range counter.

49 Kg1 e3 50 Kf1 Qf3+ 51 Kg1 ½-½

Perhaps Black should play on here, leaving the queen on a8 and instead advancing the king.

NOTE: The queen can control a diagonal from the corner of the board.

Try it Yourself

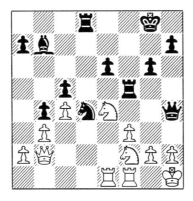

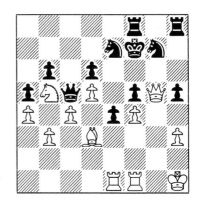

| Exercise 1 | Exercise 2 |

Exercise 1: No prizes for spotting the theme upon which Black – to move – should concentrate, but the subsequent variations are far from obvious.

Exercise 2: Can White find a way through to Black's shaky king?

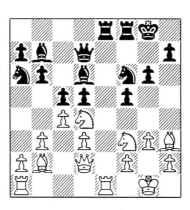

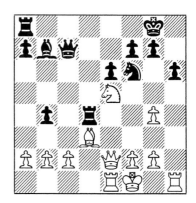

| Exercise 3 | Exercise 4 |

Exercise 3: A retreat of White's knight from d4 sees the advance of the d5-pawn, opening one long diagonal (for Black) and closing the other. How can White put his b2-bishop to very good use?

Exercise 4: White (to move) has an obvious plan in 1 g5, but how does he make use of the h-file?

Summary

A fixed pawn is an ideal target for a pawn break

Open lines can help both defenders and attackers

Consider aggressive possibilities when a bishop occupies the same diagonal as the opponent's king

A pin can be more effective than actually winning material

Chapter Four

Using the Pieces

Different players have a particular fondness for certain pieces. As a junior I played through the games of the great Nimzowitsch and consequently began to give up my bishops for knights at the earliest opportunity in the knowledge that my trusty horses would win the game. Of course this phase eventually passed (fortunately), but my appreciation of the unique quality of the knight has not diminished.

The examples in this chapter concentrate on specific characteristics of the four 'play' pieces, or rather the special implications of the qualities of a piece in specific situations that are commonly experienced in practice. By playing through these games we can better appreciate the significance of key moments and opportunities that arise in the middlegame, thus adding to our armoury of practical resources.

The Rook on the Seventh Rank

We begin with a fairly simple but impressive example of the clinical power of a rook on the seventh rank.

Game 33
□ F.Ribeiro ■ Fandino
Cuba 1995

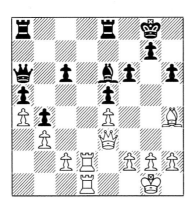

Diagram 1
Black's forces are scattered

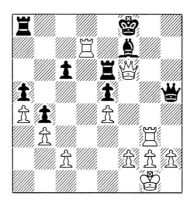

Diagram 2
White has invaded

The presence of opposite-coloured bishops combined with Black's distant queen and potentially vulnerable second rank all point to – at the very least – a search for attacking possibilities.

1 Bxf6!

Black has no influence on the dark squares so this sacrifice is quite justified.

1...gxf6

1...Bg4 2 Rd7! and 1...Bf7 2 Rd7! already demonstrate that the rook's arrival on the seventh rank takes priority over albeit temporary material considerations.

2 Rd7!

All of a sudden Black's king begins to look rather lonely as White's rook sets up mate threats.

2...Bf7

Obviously White had to check that 2...Bxd7 3 Rxd7 does indeed lead to a forced mate. With the text Black hopes to close out the rook, but he is left tied up in any case.

3 Qxh6 Qe2

Ruling out Rxf7 and preparing to transfer to the kingside. In reply to 3...Ra7 White has the ruthless 4 R7d3! with the deadly swing to the g-file.

4 Qxf6 Qh5 5 R1d3 Re6

5...Kf8 6 Rf3.

6 Rg3+ Kf8 (Diagram 2) 7 Rxf7+!

The problem for the defender when faced with an unwelcome visitor on his second rank is that pieces used to lessen the influence of the rook tend to become targets.

7...Qxf7 8 Qh8+ Ke7 9 Qxa8 1-0

Game 34
□ **Sagalchik** ■ **Akopian**
New York 1998

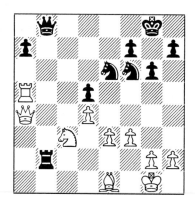

Diagram 3
White's king is surprisingly vulnerable

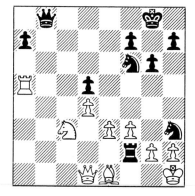

Diagram 4 (variation)
The rook is running riot

Black, to move, appears unable to profit from his well placed rook, but the long-range queen points directly at h2 and the knights are menacingly close to White's king. Again the defender's king lacks support.

1...Ng5!

Homing in on the king and introducing immediate threats to put his rook to good use.

2 f4

Closing the queen's diagonal. A simple mistake is 2 Rxa7?, inviting 2...Nxf3+ when Black's queen and rook team up. A more interesting illustration of how the rook can prove troublesome is the following: 2 Qd1 Nh3+! 3 Kh1 Rf2! (Diagram 4)

TIP: The mere presence of a rook on the seventh rank can be incredibly effective, assistance from other attacking pieces adding to its influence.

Here the rook exerts pressure on g2 and – with the queen – h2, which in turn has facilitated the arrival of the knight to the unlikely posting on h3, thus making the f2-square another option. Furthermore, after 4 Qd3 Qb2 5 Ra2 Black has 5...Rxg2! and the rook achieves the ultimate goal, e.g. 6 Ne2 Qxe2! etc. Another defensive try is to take charge of the h2-b8 diagonal with 2 Bg3, when the rook is given a new role: 2...Rb1+! 3 Nxb1 Qxb1+ 4 Kf2 Nge4+! 5 fxe4 Nxe4+ 6 Ke2 (6 Kf3 Qf1+) 6...Nc3+ and Black wins.

2...Ng4!

Black insists on hitting h2, and the e3-pawn is also under fire. Notice how Black's knights have accentuated the power of the rook.

3 Rb5

Certainly the most natural reaction to the mounting pressure on the other flank, seeking to force the removal of Black's annoying rook. Before seeing how Black reacts let us briefly investigate the alternatives:

a) 3 Nd1 Rb1 4 Rxa7 Kg7! (calm) 5 Ra8 Qb2! threatens to come to e2, and 6 Qe8 Qf2+!! is very nice!

b) 3 Nxd5 Rxg2+! is typical. Then 4 Kxg2 Qb2+ 5 Kf1 (5 Kg3 Qxh2+ 6 Kxg4 Qh3+ 7 Kg5 h6+ and Black delivers mate on e6) 5...Nxh2+ 6 Kg1 Ngf3+ 7 Kh1 Qe2 is final.

c) 3 Rxa7 also meets with 3...Rxg2+! 4 Kxg2 Qb2+ 5 Kg3 (5 Kg1 permits mate in two) 5...Qxh2+ with the same eventual mate on e6.

3...Rxg2+! (Diagram 5)

This should come as no surprise after the previous note, but Black's queen enters via a different route.

4 Kxg2 Nxe3+ 5 Kg3

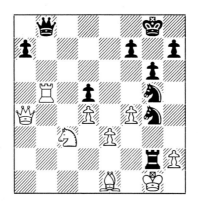

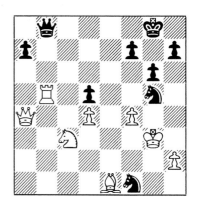

Diagram 5
White's pawn cover is blown away

Diagram 6
Black's queen forces her way in

5 Kf2 Qxf4+ 6 Ke2 Ng2!? is unpleasant for White, since after 7 Nxd5 Qe4+ 8 Kd1 Qxe1+ 9 Kc2 Nf3 White is being swamped, while 7 Bg3 Qe3+ 8 Kf1 (8 Kd1 Qd3+) 8...Qf3+ 9 Bf2 Nf4 looks decisive.

5...Nf1+! (Diagram 6) 6 Kg2

Both 6 Kf2 Qxf4+ and 6 Kg4 Qc8+ lead to forced mate.

6...Qxf4 7 Bf2 Ne3+ 8 Bxe3 Qf3+! 0-1

None of this would have been possible without the initial aggressive posting of Black's rook.

Game 35
□ **Glek** ■ **Baklan**
Berlin 1997

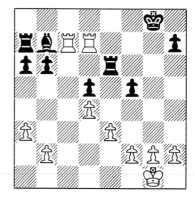

Diagram 7
White is itching to play a rook to c7

Diagram 8
The doubled rooks are decisive

The diagram position is a good example of how occupation of the only open file can be best exploited if the seventh rank is claimed. With three enemy minor pieces to attack and a potential pin to enjoy, White, to move, would like to extricate his knight from c7 and plant his rook there. It is true that no square is available but, before looking for an alternative plan, we should check all possibilities!

20 Nxe6! fxe6 21 Rc7

Notice how a single rook dominates the game.

21...Rd8

In response to 21...Rc8 White simply places his back rook on a protected square with 22 R1c3!, enabling him to maintain control of the seventh rank, and with it the game.

22 Ng5 Kg8 23 R1c3!

23 Nxe6 Rc8 is less clear, so White makes sure to keep up the pressure. In fact, with Black completely tied up, White is sure to recoup more than his initial material investment.

23...Nf5

23...e5 24 Ne6 exd4 25 exd4 Re8 26 Rxd7 Nc6 invites 27 Bxg6!, when 27...hxg6 28 Rg7+ is mate, while 27...Re7 28 Rxe7 Nxe7 29 Bxh7+ Kxh7 30 Rc7 nets White three extra pawns.

24 Nxe6 Re8 25 Rxd7 Rxe6 26 Bxf5 gxf5 27 Rcc7 (Diagram 8)

The bishop's days are numbered and White has already accumulated two pawns, with another likely to fall soon. The doubled rooks on the seventh cannot be stopped.

27...Kf8 28 Rxh7 Kg8 29 Rxb7

Of course White can subject his opponent to a little torture before cleaning up (29 g3, for example, is typically cruel), but there is nothing wrong with the text.

29...Rxb7 30 Rxb7 f4 31 Kf1 fxe3 32 fxe3 Rxe3 33 Rxb6 Rd3 34 Rxa6 Rxd4 35 Rb6 Rd2 36 a4 d4

Black's passed pawn is easily handled.

37 a5 d3 38 Ke1 Rxg2 39 a6 Kf7 40 a7 Rg1+ 41 Kd2 Ra1 42 Rb7+ Kf6 43 Kxd3 1-0

TIP: If your own piece prevents your rook from landing on the seventh rank, look for forcing ways to engineer infiltration.

Game 36
☐ **Motwani** ■ **Adams**
Moscow Olympiad 1994

White, to move, has more space, a preponderance of pawns in the centre, superior development and a well placed king. Black, meanwhile, is cramped, his rooks are yet to stir and his king cannot improve. Consequently the position is ripe for a change of pace.

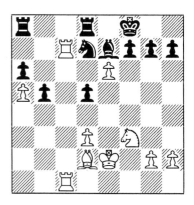

Diagram 9

White is better developed

Diagram 10

Opening up the seventh rank

18 Rc1!

White is guaranteed to make some sort of profit from his occupation of the c-file unless Black creates a target of his own pawn with 18...b4.

18...0-0

Facing facts and allowing the entry of White's rook, the alternative 18...Nb8 19 cxb5 axb5 running into 20 a6! Ra7 21 d5!, when Be3 forces a breakthrough.

19 cxb5 cxb5 20 Rc7 Rfd8 21 Rac1 Kf8

Hoping to distract White from his seventh rank mission by pushing the (passed) b-pawn has little effect: 21...b4 22 Rb7 Rab8 23 Rcc7 and now 23...b3 loses to 24 Rxd7! etc. By bringing his king closer to the centre Black can defend his minor pieces and thus release the rooks. With this in mind White now uses his presence in the centre to loosen Black's defences before consolidation is possible.

22 d5!! exd5 23 e6! (Diagram 10) 23...Nf6

After 23...fxe6 24 Nd4 White should emerge with the better game. For example 24...Bd6 25 Nxe6+ Ke7 26 Nxd8 Bxc7 27 Bg5+! Nf6 28 Rxc7+ Kxd8 29 Rxg7 wins for White, while 24...e5 25 Ne6+ Ke8 26 Rb7! is awkward to meet. However, 24...Kf7 25 Nc6 might be preferable to the game continuation, with an edge for White.

24 Ng5! h6 (Diagram 11)

24...Bd6 backfires since 25 exf7! Bxc7 26 Rxc7 forces 26...Re8+ and the subsequent loss of a piece because 26...Rd6 27 Bb4 Rad8 sees White deliver mate on e6.

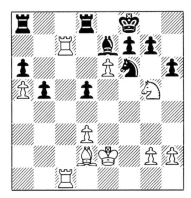

Diagram 11
White can crash through

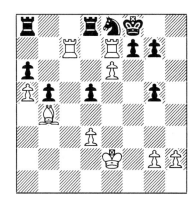

Diagram 12
White's activity is overwhelming

25 Rxe7! hxg5

25...Kxe7 26 Bb4+! Ke8 27 Rc7! and the second rook helps threaten mate in one. Then 27...fxe6 28 Re7+ (28 Nxe6? Rd7) 28...Kf8 29 Nxe6+ Kg8 30 Rxg7+ Kh8 31 Rg6 is decisive.

26 Bb4

26 Rcc7! is strong, when after the forced 26...Ne8 White then plays 27 Bb4!! **(Diagram 12)**.

A typical finish is 27...Nxc7 28 exf7!! Re8 (28...Ne8 29 Rd7+ mates) 29 Rxe8+ Kxf7 30 Re7+ etc.

26...Re8 27 Rxe8+ Kxe8 28 Rc7 fxe6 29 Re7+ Kd8 30 Rxg7 Ne8 31 Rxg5 Ra7

Material is level but White is in the driving seat. The game ended as follows: **32 Rg6 Rh7** (32...Kd7 33 h4) **33 Rxe6 Rxh2 34 Kf3 Rh4 35 Be1! Rh1 36 Bg3 Rd1? 37 Bh4+ Kd7 38 Re7+ Kc6 39 Rxe8 b4 40 Ke2 1-0**

 TIP: Once a rook is established on the seventh rank, look for ways of preventing the opponent from consolidating.

We now turn to a couple of examples of how to defend against rooks on the seventh rank.

Game 37
☐ **Barlov** ■ **Dabetic**
Yugoslavia 1994

Black's daring c2-rook is safe for the moment because its partner is ready to meet Rxc2 with a more deadly capture on e1. Consequently White sets about dealing with the unwelcome guest by providing his king with an escape square.

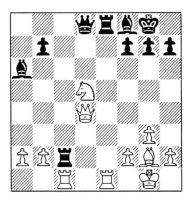

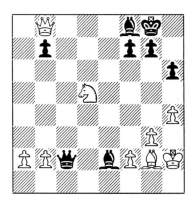

Diagram 13

The extra exchange is meaningless

Diagram 14

The rooks are gone

21 h4! Ree2

Producing a bizarre stand-off with all four rooks simultaneously defended and attacked. The aggressive 21...Bc5? backfires: 22 Rxe8+ Qxe8 23 Nf6+!. Then 23...gxf6 24 Qg4+ Kh8 25 Rxc2 is simple, which leaves 23...Kh8 24 Rxc2 Qe1+ 25 Kh2 Bxd4 26 Rc8+, and 23...Kf8 24 Nxh7+ Kg8 25 Nf6+ Kf8 26 Rxc2 Qe1+ 27 Kh2 Bxd4 28 Rc8+ Ke7 29 Re8+ etc.

22 Kh2?

White voluntarily places his king on the same rank as two(!) enemy rooks in order to concentrate on Black's vulnerable back rank. In fact it seems that, rather than dominating the game, Black's rooks are really containing White's! However, the text is – not surprisingly – suspect, and the sober 22 Rxc2 Rxe1+ (22...Rxc2 23 Ne7+) 23 Kh2 simply leaves White with a safe extra pawn.

WARNING: Double-check attractive looking variations when under pressure, especially if a simple continuation guarantees the better game.

22...Qc8?

Justifying White's audacious play. Others: 22...Rxf2? 23 Rxc2 Rxc2 24 Ne7+ and 22...Bc5? 23 Rxe2 Bxe2 (23...Bxd4 24 Rexc2) 24 Nf6+! Qxf6 25 Qxf6 gxf6 26 Rxc2 are both winning for White. However, by inserting 22...Rcd2! Black forces the queen away from the commanding d4-square, after which the capture on f2 has more sting. But fortune fa-

The Queen Sacrifice

Because the queen is the most powerful servant at our disposal we are less inclined to part with this piece than is the case with all the others. Moreover, although we are all aware that material is merely one of many factors in chess, it is only natural to allow matters of value and 'points' to invade our thought processes – which are already sufficiently complex – during this or that phase of the game. The irony is, however, that it is this very materialistic habit which often leads to certain sacrificial possibilities being overlooked.

TIP: The manner in which the queen leaves the arena can be more important than its role *on* the board.

Game 39
☐ Y.Perez ■ T.Martinez
Cuba 1994

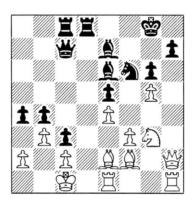

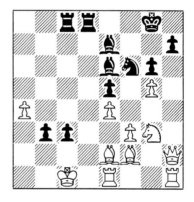

Diagram 17
How can Black break through?

Diagram 18
Black is a whole queen down!

In the diagram position Black is under considerable pressure on the h-file, particularly in view of the fact that his knight is attacked. Over on the queenside, meanwhile, White's king is by no means secure but, being the player with the threat, this seems irrelevant.

1...axb3!

The first of a series of uncompromising, brutal counterpunches from Black, deflecting attention away from his own king.

2 cxb3

Not 2 gxf6? b2+ 3 Kb1 Bxa2+ 4 Kxa2 Qa5+ etc.

2...Qa5

The threat of mate in two again forces White to postpone proceedings on the other wing.

3 a4

No doubt part of White's calculations when conducting the kingside attack that led to the diagram position. Despite his advanced pawns Black seems to have come to a standstill, with the queen locked out and even being obstructed by a friendly pawn after 3...bxa3, thus presenting White with time to snap up the knight. Nevertheless, Black now demonstrates an admirable 'liberal' attitude – assuming, of course, that it is all part of the grand plan.

3...Qxa4!!

Once again Black threatens mate, but he also loses a queen.

4 bxa4 b3! (Diagram 18)

Not much has changed since we joined the game, but the situation is no longer the same. Now White's king is under the greater pressure (see the lines in the next note) and, once White has got over the shock of seeing his (extra) queen suddenly denied the promised booty on h7, what should he play?

5 Bc5

One of a number of tries, none of which stems the tide, e.g. 5 gxf6 Ba3+ 6 Kb1 c2+; and 5 Kb1 Ba3! 6 Bd1 Rxd1+! 7 Rxd1 c2+, with mate in both cases. Another desperate plea for mercy is 5 Bd3 Rxd3 6 Bc5 Bxc5 7 Re2 to defend along the second rank, but then a quick points update after 7...Ba3+ 8 Kb1 c2+ 9 Rxc2 bxc2+ 10 Qxc2 Rxc2 11 Kxc2 Rxf3 puts White in distant second place.

5...Bxc5 6 Bd1 Ba3+ 7 Kb1 Rxd1+! 8 Rxd1 c2+ 9 Qxc2 bxc2+ 10 Ka1 Rb8!?

Cheeky.

11 Rb1 Rxb1+ 12 Rxb1 cxb1Q+ 13 Kxb1 Nh5 0-1

(So the knight does move, eventually!). Definitely one to remember – Black's forces were able to create enough threats, and subsequently finish off the game, without the help of the queen. However, only through an appreciation of how the queen can be fully utilised is it possible to find oneself in such a situation.

As I mentioned earlier (and elsewhere) there is more to chess than the material aspect. Of equal – if not greater – importance is the harmony of the pieces. What use is a queen, for example, if it does not combine well with the rest of the workforce? And with this in mind, why not part with the queen for a couple of your opponent's most promising pieces if this in turn accentuates the influence of your own? Here is a good illustration of this approach.

Game 40
☐ **Bratchenko** ■ **Motylev**
St Petersburg 1997

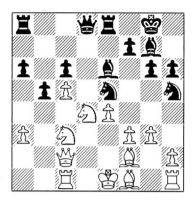

Diagram 19

Black's minor pieces now come to life

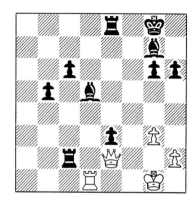

Diagram 20

Black's pieces are rampant

White is lagging behind in development but at least he is in possession of a commanding knight in the centre to match its counterpart on e5, which can be evicted by a timely push of the f-pawn.

21...Qxd4!

Not any more, he doesn't!

22 Bxd4 Nxf3+ 23 Kf2 Nxd4

Keeping an eye on the 'points' situation, for his queen Black has collected a strong knight, an important bishop and a pawn, so in terms of the score White should have the better of the deal. However, Black's dark-squared bishop can now operate unchallenged, his knight has a more advanced posting, the e4-pawn lacks proper support and, crucially, White's army has lost three members compared to only one from Black. The queen is a strong piece, but it is also a *single* piece. As if to reiterate this fact White already finds his own queen under fire.

24 Qb2 Nf6

Returning the knight to the fold and reminding White of his new responsibility on e4.

25 Kg2?!

In view of what happens 25 Bd3 might be better, when Black can introduce his final piece into the game with 25...Rad8, go for the c5-pawn as in the game or plant a knight on the wonderful e5-square.

25...Nb3 26 Re1 Nxc5

Adding to the collection. Note how White's forces lack that all-important harmony whereas Black's seem like close friends!

27 Qb4

Removing the queen from the firing line of Black's mighty bishop, which grew in stature as soon as White's dark-squared bishop left the board. White has not had time to influence any of the play since Black's queen sacrifice, being obliged instead to find safe squares for his queen and rook.

27...Nfxe4!

Thanks to the coming pin Black is able to further infiltrate White's camp and grab another pawn in the process.

28 Nxe4 Nxe4 29 Rxe4

Not an easy choice to make, but 29 Bd3 Ng5 is terrible for White.

29...Bd5

Pin it and win it.

30 Bd3 f5 31 Rd1 Rad8!? 32 Bc2 fxe4 33 Kg1

White has finally regrouped what pieces he has left, but there is nothing for him to attack – a problem that cannot be said of Black.

33...a5!? 34 Qxa5 e3 35 Bd3 Ra8 36 Qe1

Or 36 Qb4 Ra4.

36...Rxa3 37 Qe2

37 Bxg6 e2! 38 Rxd5! cxd5 39 Bxe8 Ra1 40 Kf2 offers White drawing chances, but 38...Ra1! 39 Kf2 Rxe1 40 Bxe8 Ra1 wins for Black.

37...Ra2 38 Bc2 Rxc2! 0-1 (Diagram 20)

After 39 Qxc2 e2 40 Re1 Black delivers mate on d4. White's queen seemed no more than a liability from the moment its opposite number stole the show.

Game 41
□ **Sakaev** ■ **Rublevsky**
Russian Ch 1998

This time White judges that with the d5-bishop cemented in the middle of the board his best practical chance of exploiting his superior forces and the protected passed pawn involves a queen sacrifice.

(Diagram 21) 1 Qxd5!? exd5 2 Nxf5

Unlike the previous example Black has few weaknesses and White has fewer pieces. Consequently the subsequent focus of the struggle is easier for both sides to determine, a key feature being the untouchable d6-pawn.

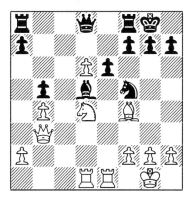

Diagram 21
White activates the minor pieces...

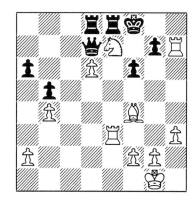

Diagram 22
White's activity is overwhelming

TIP: A major aim of a long-term queen sacrifice is to unsettle the opponent, who often finds himself – thanks to reduced resources – at a loss for a plan.

Of course inflicting this psychological blow is a decent bonus, and here Black fails to address the invading pieces accurately.

2...Re8?!

The beginning of a faulty plan. The suggested improvement 2...Qd7 3 Rxd5 f6 4 h3! (4 Re7 Rfe8 and White's back rank is a problem) 4...Rfe8 5 Ne7+ Kf7 is a little better for White after 6 Rc5, when the attempt to break out and generate counterplay on the wing with 6...a5? 7 bxa5 Rxa5 might be asking for trouble after 8 Rc7 etc.

3 Ne7+ Kf8?

Neither square looks appealing but this helps White. The lesser evil is 3...Kh8 4 Rxd5 Qd7 5 h3.

4 Rxd5 Qd7 5 h3 a6

5...f6 6 Rc5 is easier to play for White. In fact this is generally the case since Black has only major pieces, while White's assortment of pieces – together with the enormous d-pawn (the b4-pawn is also useful) – offers much more versatility.

6 Rh5! f6

6...h6 7 Rxh6! is not an easy one to spot!

7 Rxh7 Rad8

7...Kf7 8 Bh6.

8 Re3 (Diagram 22)

It is clear from a brief appraisal of this position that the 'schoolboy' points value of the pieces by no means automatically translates to actual value on the board. The knight is arguably the most influential piece here, but an exchange sacrifice is out of the question because this brings White's rook to the seventh rank.

8...Rc8

What else?

9 Nxc8 Kg8

9...Rxe3 10 Rh8+ leaves the queen in a hopeless situation, while 9...Rxc8 10 Re7 is final.

10 Nb6

The beginning of the end.

10...Qd8 11 Rxe8+ Qxe8 12 d7 Qd8 13 Rh5 g5

Hoping to close out the rook. Instead 13...Qxb6 loses to 14 Rd5 Qd8 15 Bc7.

14 Be3 Kg7 15 h4 Kg6 16 Rxg5+! 1-0

Bishops versus Knights

We all know that knights have an advantage over bishops in blocked positions and that bishops favour more open situations. However, while the former is fairly simple to appreciate because knights can hop about while poor bishops suffocate, making the most of bishops in 'normal' (i.e. not closed) positions can be problematic. This is because the knights tend to be free to move around, too, if not to the same extent as the bishops. There is a tendency, as soon as we find ourselves the proud owners of bishops against our opponents' lowly knights, to immediately go active. However, a patient approach has a better chance of success.

Let us see how Kasparov handled this situation against his future nemesis Kramnik.

Game 42
□ **Kasparov** ■ **Kramnik**
Linares 1997

We join the game at a stage where the bishops are having a problem making their presence felt, the symmetry and the d3-rook compounding White's efforts. Kasparov begins by evicting the rook.

(Diagram 23) 27 Rb4 Rxc3 28 Rxc4 Rxc4 29 Qxc4 Qb8?

The removal of the c-pawns has already changed the character of the game a little by opening the queenside, and this prompts Black's first error. In fact the direct 29...Qxa5! 30 Qxc8+ Kh7 31 Rb1 Rb6 pins and wins the bishop in view of 32 Bd3 Rxb1+ 33 Bxb1 Qe1+ etc. Instead White should continue 32 Qf5+ Kg8 33 Qxe5 (33 Rc1 Qxb5 34 Rc8+ Ne8 35 Qxe5 Qxe5 36 Bxe5 Re6) 33...a6 34 Bh4 Rxb5 35 Rxb5 axb5 36 Bxf6 gxf6 37 Qxf6, although 37...Qe1+ 38 Kh2 Qxe4 39 Qxh6 b4 seems to draw. This line, of course, is difficult to calculate during a game – even for the top players – and so Kramnik plays safe. The downside to the game continuation is Black's gradual drift into passivity, but the onus is still on White to demonstrate a worthwhile advantage.

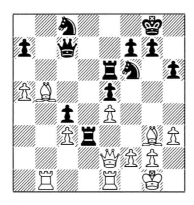

Diagram 23

Black is active but White has bishops

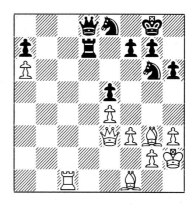

Diagram 24

White plays patiently

30 Qc5! Nd6 31 Bd3 Nd7

Gaining time on the queen to redeploy the knight on g6, thus monitoring the f4-square (and h4) in anticipation of White eventually dropping his bishop back to the more profitable g1–a7 diagonal.

32 Qa3 Nf8 33 Rb1 Qc7 34 Rc1 Qd8 35 a6!?

Fixing the pawn on a7, where it should prove a juicy target. Notice that White is in no rush to actually use his bishops yet, opting instead to improve his queen and rook and sort out where he wants the pawns.

35...Ng6 36 Qc5 Re7 37 f3 Ne8 38 Bf1 Rc7 39 Qe3 Rd7

White is happy to trade rooks because he still has a bishop and queen with which to attack a7, but Black's rook is a useful defender.

40 Kh2! (Diagram 24)

Another instructive move from Kasparov. It may not be necessary to lodge the king on h2, but at least there is no need to worry about inconvenient back rank checks in any variations, checks on the g1–a7 diagonal (unlikely considering who has the bishop) or a knight check on e2.

40...Re7 41 Rc6

41 Rb1! is stronger, eyeing the entry point on b7. However, by conducting the game in such a patient fashion White, with no weaknesses, should be able to regroup and then induce the necessary concession on the queenside. Black is reduced to improving his pieces the best he can while keeping guard over the a7-pawn.

41...Kh7 42 Qc1 Nc7 43 Qc3! Qd7 44 Rc5 Qd6 45 Bf2 (Diagram 25)

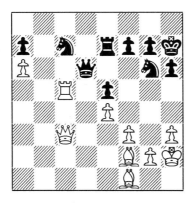

Diagram 25
White targets the a7-pawn

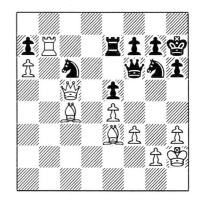

Diagram 26
White is closing in

Finally! The long-range bishops, from the safety of home ground, both defend and attack the relevant pawns.

45...Ne6 46 Rd5 Qb8 47 Rb5! Qd6 48 Rb7!

Now each of White's pieces is working at near maximum capacity.

48...Nd4 49 Qb4 Qf6

After the exchange of queens White simply returns the rook to b7.

50 Qc5 Nc6 51 Be3

Just in case Black wants to check on f4. Note that since White has stepped up the pressure Black's options have been diminishing.

51...Re6 52 Bc4 Re7 (Diagram 26) 53 Bd5

Also good is 53 Bxf7 Rxf7 54 Rxf7 Qxf7 55 Qxc6, e.g. 55...Qb3 56 Qc5, or 55...Qa2 56 Qb5 Nh4 57 Qf1 etc.

53...Nd4 54 Rxa7 Rxa7 55 Qxa7 Ne7 56 Bc4 h5

56...Qc6 57 Bxd4 exd4 58 Qxe7 Qxc4 59 a7 Qa6 60 Qxf7 d3 61 Qf5+ is another way to lose.

57 Qc5 1-0

TIP: Patience is paramount with bishops versus knights – concentrate on the rest of your forces, too, with a view to ultimately creating a multi-piece zugzwang.

Understanding the superiority of a 'good' knight versus 'bad' bishop is not too taxing, but being alert to the possibilities of engineering such a situation is another matter.

Game 43
□ **Mortensen** ■ **Petursson**
Copenhagen 1997

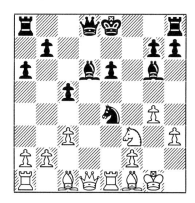

Diagram 27
Which king is more exposed?

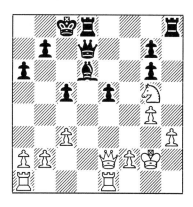

Diagram 28
e4 is a great square for White

One of our first thoughts on glancing at Diagram 27 might be a slightly worrying one from White's side of the board: can the kingside structure be exploited by Black? Another might concern the e-file, namely the isolated e-pawn (long-term weakness), Black's king (short-term vulnerability) and the e4-knight, which must be evicted. In fact White would like to establish a knight on e4, from where it could survey both sides of the board and blockade the e-pawn.

17 Bg5!

Your opponent will not voluntarily exchange pieces in order to leave himself with a bad bishop against a good knight. It is necessary to bring about the situation yourself, and this can be achieved by anticipating an opportunity (for either side) to challenge or exchange pieces with a view to removing the desired ones. Incidentally 17 Bd3 0-0 18 Bxe4?! Bxe4 19 Rxe4?? Bh2+ drops the queen.

17...Qd7

The obvious 17...Nxg5 18 Nxg5 0-0 (18...Qxg5 19 Qxd6) 19 Nxe6 Qf6

20 Qxd6 Qxf2+ 21 Kh1 simply loses Black a piece.

18 Bd3 Nxg5 19 Bxg6+

19 Nxg5?? Bxd3 20 Qxd3 Bh2+ is another way for White to lose his queen.

19...hxg6

19...Nf7?? 20 Bxf7+ Kxf7 21 Ne5+.

20 Nxg5 0-0-0 21 Qe2

White is not interested – for the moment – in taking the e-pawn, preferring to stamp his positional superiority on the game by concentrating on the light squares.

21...e5 22 Kg2 (Diagram 28)

This is exactly the set-up White was aiming for when he began the initial minor piece exchange.

22...Be7

22...Qc6+ is a waste of time since 23 Qe4 proposes a queen trade that is favourable to White.

23 Ne4

Avoiding the disastrous 23 Nf7? Qd5+ 24 Qf3 Qxf3+ 25 Kxf3 Rhf8, but 23 Nf3!? Bf6 24 Rad1 Qc6 25 Rxd8+ Rxd8 26 Qe4 is very pleasant for White. Nevertheless, it is simpler to post the knight on the more natural e4-square, directly in front of the pawn (which is a permanent weakness and can be targeted later) and monitoring c5, d6 and f6.

23...Qd3

23...Qc6 24 Rad1.

24 Qxd3 Rxd3 25 Re3!? Rxe3 26 fxe3

It might seem odd to accept an isolated pawn in this way, but now the f4-square is protected and White also covers d4 in case it becomes advantageous to push the c-pawn.

26...Kd7

26...c4 prevents White's next but runs into 27 Rd1, e.g. 27...Rd8 28 Rxd8+ Kxd8 29 Nd2 b5 30 Kf3 Kd7 31 Ke4 Ke6 32 Nf3 Bd6 33 Ng5+ Kf6 34 Kd5! etc.

27 c4! Ke6 28 a4 Rb8 29 Ra3 b5 30 Rb3 b4 31 Rd3 b3

Otherwise White will have all but the untouchable e3-pawn on light squares: 31...Rc8 32 b3 Rc7 33 Rd5 Rc8 34 Nd2 Rf8 35 Nf3 Bd6 36 Ng5+ Ke7 37 Ne4 Rd8 38 Kf3.

32 Nd2 Rb4 33 Kf3!

The b3-pawn is going nowhere and White wants to gain control of e4.

33...Rxa4 34 Rxb3 Rb4 35 Rxb4 cxb4 36 Nb3 Kd6 37 Ke4 Bd8

Now White could have crowned a well-played game with **38 Nd2 a5 39 b3 Bf6 40 Nf3**, when both **40...a4 41 bxa4 b3 42 Nd2 b2 43 Kd3 Kc5 44 a5** and **40...Ke6 41 Ne1 Kd6 42 Nd3** are decisive.

In fact White played **38 Nc1? a5 39 b3**, allowing a draw after **39...a4! 40 bxa4 Kc5** etc. (Black played **39...Bh4?** and went on to lose).

As soon as White was able to establish the good knight versus bad bishop scenario the game became rather easy to play.

TIP: When contemplating exchange sequences be on the lookout for the chance to emerge with the superior minor piece. Remember that for most players it is natural to want bishop v. knight, and any positional downside to this might become apparent once it is too late.

Opposite-Coloured Bishops

The very nature of opposite-coloured bishop middlegames calls for active, alert play. Often the first player to generate an initiative holds a sizeable advantage because the defender has difficulty contesting the attacker's bishop. We tend to see a unique situation in which the players seem to operate exclusively of each other, one concentrating on the dark squares and the other on light squares – not surprisingly this usually leads to a decision!

Game 44
□ **Leko** ■ **A.Rodriguez**
Yopal 1997

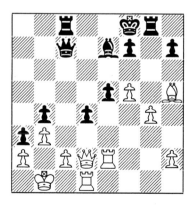

Diagram 29
Who has the better bishop?

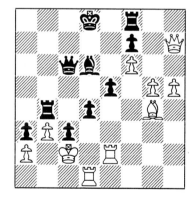

Diagram 30
White plans a kingside push

Even the pawns have got in on the act here, with the board bizarrely split into two colour complexes. For the moment the material situation takes a supporting role, with the initiative (i.e. generally creating utmost inconvenience for the opponent) being paramount.

26 f6!

A good start. White guarantees either a closer presence to Black's king or the opening of the f-file.

26...Bd6

26...Bxf6 27 Rf1 is exactly what White is looking for.

27 Qh6+ Ke8

Now 28 Qxh7 Qc3! is a typical stand-off that leads to a draw after either 29 Qxf7+ Kd8 30 Qxg8+ Kd7 31 Qh7+ Kc6 or 29 Rxe5+ Kd7 30 Qxf7+ Kc6 31 Qd5+ Kc7 32 Qa5+ Kd7 etc. Another wild line is 28 Rxd4 Qc3! 29 Rxe5+ Kd8! (29...Bxe5 30 Bxf7+! Kxf7 31 Qxh7+ Kxf6 32 Qf5+ mates, and 29...Kd7 30 Re7+ Kc6 31 Rc4+ wins for White) 30 Rxd6+ Kc7 31 Re7+ Kxd6 32 Qf4+ Kc6 with a messy position.

28 c4!!

Whatever happens next White no longer has to worry about the prospect of Black's queen coming to c3 with a nasty mate threat. Consequently White is free to continue his attack. Leko's thematic concentration of play on the light squares is instructive.

28...bxc3 29 Kc2 Kd8 30 Qxh7 Rf8 31 g5!

Releasing the hitherto dormant bishop which, ironically, has played no part in White's exclusive light square treatment.

31...Rb8 32 Bg4 Qc6 33 h4!

Without a single entry square available to Black's queen White sets his pawns rolling, the simple threat now being their continued advance.

33...Rb4

After 33...Kc7 34 g6 the self-pin facilitates the march.

34 h5! (Diagram 30) 34...d3+!?

A good practical try. Otherwise White simply pushes on and trades in a pawn for a rook.

35 Qxd3 Rd4

35...Rxg4 36 Qxd6+ Qxd6 37 Rxd6+ Kc7 38 Rd5 Rxg5 39 Rdxe5 and White wins the ending.

36 Qf5 Rd2+

36...Rxd1 37 Kxd1 alters nothing.

37 Rexd2 cxd2+ 38 Kxd2 Kc7

38...Qg2+ 39 Ke3 Qg3+ 40 Ke4 Qg2+ 41 Kd3 does not help Black, e.g. 41...Qg3+ 42 Kc4.

39 Bf3 Bb4+ 40 Ke2 e4

Black, short of time and in an anyway hopeless situation, hopes for 41 Qxe4?? Re8.

41 Bxe4 1-0

TIP: When the opposite-coloured bishops are the only minor pieces left, make an effort to operate exclusively on 'your' colour complex.

Game 45
□ **Hector** ■ **Krasenkov**
Malmö 1995

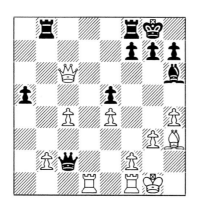

Diagram 31
Who will get active first?

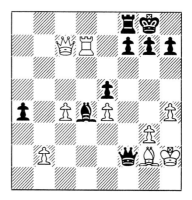

Diagram 32
Black has a huge bishop

Here we have a more sober layout of pawns, but the opposite-coloured bishops eventually take the game into uncharted territory. As was mentioned earlier, the side to first activate his bishop sets the pace. At the moment both bishops occupy the 'same' square, but Black has the move and a nice incidental tactic to assume the advantage.

24...Be3!

Exploiting White's vulnerable second rank to transform the bishop to monster status. The immediate 24...Rxb2 allows White to do the same with 25 Rd7!, when the f7-pawn is as weak as its opposite number on f2.

25 Rd7!

Fighting for activity of his own before the route is closed. Obviously

White should avoid 25 fxe3?? Rxb2 etc.

25...Bd4

As per plan. The flashy 25...Rxb2? is deservedly punished after 26 Rxf7! when the tables are turned on Black.

26 Qc7 Rb3!

Already we see how Black's newly arrived bishop plays the starring role in the game. Apart from the obvious pressure on the f2-pawn Black, through the pin on the g1–a7 diagonal, threatens the g3-pawn.

27 Kh1! Rf3!?

Black prefers to pursue the theme of play on the dark squares rather than grab the e4-pawn, which leads to unclear play after 27...Qxe4+ 28 Bg2 Qf5 29 Rd8 g6 30 Rxf8+ Kxf8 31 Qxa5 Rxb2 32 f4! etc.

28 Bg2 Rxf2 29 Rxf2 Qxf2 30 Kh2 a4! (Diagram 32)

For good reason Black is not prepared to part with this pawn, the promotion square being on the same diagonal as the all-seeing bishop. And herein lies the problem for White – the major difference between the two sides is that of the bishops, Black's contributing to mate threats and adding weight to the a-pawn while White's is a spectator.

31 Rd8 g6 32 Rxf8+ Kxf8 33 Qb8+?

Yet another example of a careless check helping the opponent. Much better is the immediate 33 c5 Qxb2 34 c6 Kg7 since Black's king should leave the back rank in any case to rule out a tempo-gaining check. Then 35 Qb7 a3 36 Qxb2 axb2 37 c7 b1Q 38 c8Q gives Black an extra pawn and the better pieces but at least it is preferable to what happens in the game.

33...Kg7 34 c5 Qc2! 35 Qe8 Bxb2 36 c6 a3 (Diagram 33)

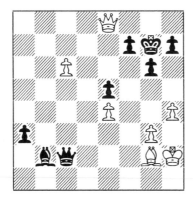

Diagram 33
Racing to promote

Diagram 34
Black still has the better bishop

Prepare to be confused...

37 Qa8

37 Qd7 a2 38 c7 a1Q 39 c8Q Qf2 wins for Black.

37...h5?

With both players doing their utmost to promote/hold back pawns, a kingside distraction will be imperative – hence the text. However, 37...Qc3! 38 Qa6 Bc1! 39 Qa8 h5 is more accurate.

38 Qa6 Qc3 39 Qa8?

The best chance to hold is 39 Bf1!! Bc1 40 Qc4! Qd2+ 41 Bg2 a2 42 Qa4!.

39...Bc1!

To be fair to White his opponent's kingside plan is difficult to spot.

40 Qb7

After 40 Qa6 g5! we see what Black has in mind: 41 hxg5 h4 42 c7 hxg3+ 43 Kh3 Qxc7 steals the c-pawn and with it White's hopes of holding the game.

TIP: It might be necessary to use your greater influence on a particular colour complex on one flank in order to push home an advantage on the other.

40...a2

Hector's proposed 40...Bf4!? is worth investigating: 41 gxf4 exf4 42 c7 Qg3+ 43 Kh1 f3 44 Bxf3 Qxf3+ 45 Kg1 Qd1+ 46 Kf2 Qd2+ 47 Kf3 a2 48 Qa7 Qc3+ 49 Ke2 Qb2+ 50 Ke3 a1Q 51 Qxa1 Qxa1 52 c8Q Qe1+ and Black wins the queen ending.

41 c7 a1Q 42 c8Q (Diagram 34)

Not the kind of position we see every day! Notice that, as if to emphasise the theme, the queens all stand on the 'appropriate' colour complex. The golden rule that the first player to make a telling strike holds all the cards still applies here, and Black, still with the (far) superior bishop, has the move.

42...Qxg3+!

How many queens does Black need to stamp his authority on the dark squares? With White's so far away they could be in another game it appears that one should be sufficient.

43 Kxg3 Bf4+ 44 Kf2

44 Kf3 Qd1+ transposes.

44...Qd4+ 45 Kf1 Qd1+ 46 Kf2 Qd2+ 47 Kf1

47 Kg1 Qe1+ 48 Bf1 Qg3+ 49 Bg2 Be3+ 50 Kh1 Qe1+ 51 Kh2 Bf4+ mates.

47...Bg3!

Threatening mates on f2 and e1 and therefore prompting desperate measures from White. The game finished **48 Qxf7+ Kxf7 49 Qc4+ Kg7 50 Kg1 Qe1+ 51 Qf1 Bxh4 52 Qxe1 Bxe1 53 Bf3 Kh6 0-1**

A wonderful 'how to play' example.

By adding a pair of knights the nature of the game is not so intense, the knights' versatility adding to the mix an opportunity to both accentuate the concentration on one colour complex and combine with play on the other colour. Watch how Karpov transforms his bishop and subsequently causes havoc on the light squares.

Game 46
□ **Karpov** ■ **J.Polgar**
Dos Hermanas 1997

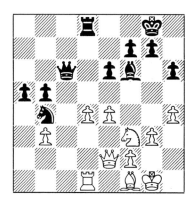

Diagram 35
How does White activate the bishop?

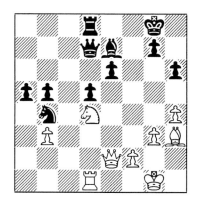

Diagram 36
White has powerful light-square play

26 d5! exd5 27 e5 Be7

27...Re8 28 Qxb5 favours White since 28...Bxe5? loses to 29 Qxc6 Nxc6 30 Bb5.

28 Nd4 Qd7

28...Qe8 29 Qg4! is given by Karpov.

29 e6 fxe6 30 Bh3 (Diagram 36)

The double pawn sacrifice is only temporary and, when White redresses the material balance, the initiative created on the light squares is difficult for Black to address. Note that White is helped in his campaign by his superior knight, which monitors the key squares b5, c6, e6 and f5.

30...Qe8 31 Qxe6+ Qf7 32 Qb6 Kh8 33 Qxb5 Ra8!

Holding the a-pawn is preferable to the ineffectual 33...Rf8 34 Rf1.

34 Re1 Bf6 35 Nf5 Qf8 36 Re6 d4 37 Bg4?!

White misses 37 Nd6! d3 38 Qh5! d2 39 Bf5, using his domination of the light squares to generate threats against Black's king, e.g. 39...Rd8 40 Kg2!, when Black's pawn is ready to queen and the d6-knight is hanging, but her light squares are dismally lacking in defence. A sample line is 40...Kg8 41 Qg6 Rxd6 42 Re8 Be7 (42...d1Q 43 Qh7+ Kf7 44 Bg6 mate) 43 Be6+ Kh8 44 Rxf8+ Bxf8 45 Qf7 Rxe6 46 Qxf8+ Kh7 47 Qd8. With the text Karpov uses his bishop – and, subsequently, his rook – to monitor the d-pawn rather than all-out attack, thus presenting his opponent with an opportunity to get back in the game.

37...d3 38 Bh5 d2 39 Rd6 Rd8 40 Rxd8 Qxd8 41 Ne3

Not 41 Nd6? d1Q+.

41...Nd3 42 Nd1 Ne5 43 Ne3

43 Be2?! meets with 43...Qa8! followed by the check on f3.

43...Nd3 44 Qf5 Nb2 45 Nd1 Nxd1 46 Bxd1 Kg8

The game ended as follows: **47 Qe6+ Kf8 48 Kg2 Qe7 49 Qc8+ Qd8 50 Qc5+ Kg8 51 Qc4+ Kh8 52 Qe4 Qe7 53 Qf5 Qd8 54 Kf1 Qa8 55 Ke2 Qa6+ 56 Kxd2 Qd6+ 57 Kc1 Qa3+ 58 Kd2 Qd6+ 59 Ke2 Qe5+ 60 Qxe5 Bxe5 ½-½**

Try it Yourself

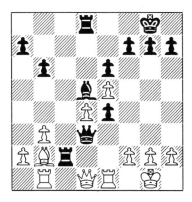

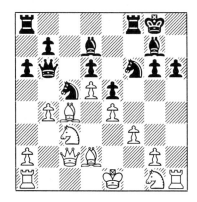

Exercise 1 **Exercise 2**

Exercise 1: Black has a commanding position but how can his c2-rook help net the full point?

Exercise 2: Should Black accept the b4-pawn?

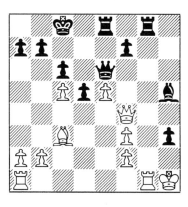

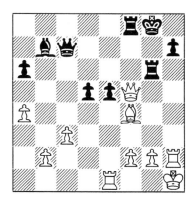

Exercise 3 **Exercise 4**

Exercise 3: How can Black crown his domination of the light squares?

Exercise 4: 1 Qxe5 Qxe5 2 Bxe5 Rxf2 is not clear, but White has a better try.

Summary

A rook on the seventh rank can be devastating

The queen's versatility allows for special sacrificial options unavailable to other pieces

Patience is the key when holding bishops against knights

The initiative is paramount in opposite-coloured bishop middlegames

Chapter Five

Using the Pawns

Pawns probably receive the least respect from most players, yet these loyal foot soldiers deserve to be treated with care. In terms of movement pawns are severely restricted, yet they can be very useful indeed, the task altering as the game progresses, with the ultimate reward to a respectful owner being the transformation to a new queen.

In this chapter we investigate several themes that are encountered frequently in practice. First are two illustrations of the exploitation of standard structural features.

Structural Strengths and Weaknesses

Game 47
☐ **Moroz** ■ **G.Timoshenko**
Enakievo 1997

1 e4 e5 2 Nf3 Nc6 3 d4 exd4 4 Nxd4 Bc5 5 Nxc6 Qf6 6 Qd2 dxc6

For decent development Black accepts doubled pawns, thus presenting White with an early advantage in the form of an unhindered kingside pawn majority. Note that in this case, unlike the Exchange variation of the Ruy Lopez (1 e4 e5 2 Nf3 Nc6 3 Bb5 a6 4 Bxc6 dxc6), White has not had to part with a bishop for the privilege.

7 Nc3 Ne7 8 Qf4 Be6 9 Qxf6 gxf6

Again Black has invited the creation of doubled pawns in order to get on with development. The f6-pawn can challenge the e4-pawn, but Black will still have three pawn islands to White's two. Theoretically, of course, this variation is not necessarily unsound for Black, but from a practical viewpoint it is easy to drift into a poor position.

10 Na4!? Bb4+ 11 c3 Bd6 12 Be3 (Diagram 1)

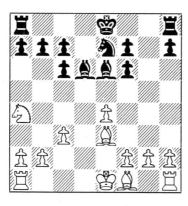 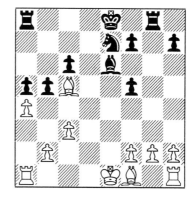

Diagram 1
Black's pawns are ragged

Diagram 2
White attacks the weaknesses

The exchanges have helped the game along to the early middlegame phase. Now the struggle concentrates on the pawn structures.

12...f5

Contesting the centre before White consolidates, e.g. 12...Rg8 13 f4 with a clear advantage to White.

13 Bd4 Rg8

After 13...f6 14 Bxf6 Rf8 15 Bd4! fxe4 16 Nc5 Black's structure might be even worse.

14 e5

Forcing an interesting mini-skirmish of pawns from which Black trades in one positional disadvantage for another.

14...b5 15 exd6 cxd6 16 Nc5 dxc5 17 Bxc5 a5 18 a4! (Diagram 2)

White continues to exert pressure on the enemy pawns before Black pushes his own pawn to a4. The text is guaranteed to create further weaknesses that White's bishop pair should later combine to exploit. Note that, thus far, White has been careful not to commit his own pawns – a completely contrasting approach to Black, who seems to have few worries about their well-being.

18...bxa4

Black is stuck between a rock and a hard place! 18...b4 19 cxb4 axb4 20 a5 releases the a-pawn and weakens the b-pawn. The text, meanwhile, leaves Black with four pawn islands!

19 Rxa4 Rg4!? 20 Rxg4!?

White grants his opponent's wish to 'correct' the kingside pawns rather than fix them with 20 f4 Nd5 21 g3 Kd7, when Black is definitely worse but is still in the game.

20...fxg4 21 h3! gxh3

Now White played the incredulous 22 gxh3?, after which 22...Rd8 23 Rg1 Rd5 24 Be3 Nf5 allowed Black to activate his pieces and subsequently keep the disadvantage to a minimum, eventually earning a draw. Having stressed the importance of the need to keep one's pawns intact whenever possible, it makes sense for White to adhere to this maxim – as he has done admirably thus far – and there is a means to do just that.

22 g3! Rd8 23 Bxh3 leaves Black with very weak pawns, while White's can be solidly protected. After 23...Bd5 24 0-0!? White's rook is ready to make its presence felt, although the h-file is a decent home, too, as the h-pawn is a juicy target. Perhaps Black's best is **23...Rd5 24 Ba3 Rh5 25 Bg2 Rxh1+ 26 Bxh1**. However, White has excellent winning chances whether or not Black cancels out the bishop pair with 26...Bd5.

WARNING: Structural weaknesses in the opening have a nasty habit of staying with you through the middlegame and into the ending!

Game 48
□ **Kramnik** ■ **Svidler**
Dortmund 1998

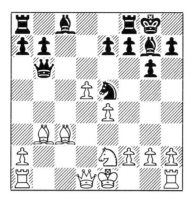

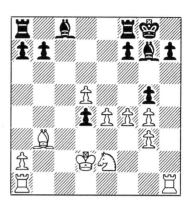

Diagram 3
White gets the centre pawns going

Diagram 4
White keeps the pawns intact

Here we have another example of a game that quickly weaves through the opening, middlegame and ending stages. Already with a greater influence in the centre, Kramnik decides to put his faith in his advanced pawns.

1 f4!

The first part of a forcing continuation that is designed to steer the game into a queenless middlegame in which White's centre pawns dominate.

1...Ng4 2 Bd4 Qa5+

2...Bxd4 3 Qxd4 Qxd4 4 Nxd4 merely improves White's knight.

3 Qd2 Qxd2+ 4 Kxd2 e5?!

The circumspect 4...Rd8 is superior to the text, which brings about an alteration of the respective pawn structures that results in the accentuation of White's central presence.

5 h3!

White both parts with his bishop and prepares a pawn sacrifice, judging that the pawns on the two centre files will be too strong.

5...exd4

No doubt part of the plan, although there is no choice anyway since

5...Nf6 6 fxe5 Nxe4+ 7 Ke3 is much worse, e.g. 7...Bf5 (or 7...f5 8 d6+ etc.) 8 g4 Bh6+ 9 Nf4.

6 hxg4 g5

6...Bxg4 7 e5 Bxe2 8 Kxe2 is similar to the game, while 6...d3 7 Nc3 Bxg4 8 Kxd3 Rac8 9 Rac1 is very pleasant for White.

7 g3! (Diagram 4)

White consistently keeps his pawn mass intact.

7...Bxg4

White's armada of pawns is so impressive that he might consider answering 7...d3 8 Nc3 Bxg4 9 Kxd3 Bf3 with 10 e5!? Bxh1 11 Rxh1, when the position is by no means suitable for Black's rooks and the g7-bishop is closed out.

8 e5 Bxe2 9 Kxe2

With rooks and opposite-coloured bishops on the board White's winning chances increase and, while the b3-bishop will come to life once the d-pawn clears the a2-g8 diagonal by advancing one step closer to promotion, the prospects of Black's bishop, locked in by a wall of white pawns, are poor.

9...Rfc8 10 Rad1 Rc3 11 Rd3 Rac8

The immediate 11...b5 looks better because this rook ultimately hastens the end.

12 d6 b5

12...Rxd3 13 Kxd3 Rc3+ 14 Kxd4 Rxg3 15 d7 wins for White.

13 Rxc3! dxc3

Not 13...Rxc3?? 14 d7.

14 e6!

This inevitable advance puts the key players side by side and guarantees White a decisive material gain.

14...Kf8

14...Bf8 15 e7 Bxe7 16 dxe7 Re8 17 fxg5 Rxe7+ 18 Kd3 wins easily for White.

15 e7+ Ke8 16 Bxf7+! 1-0

A fitting finale, as one of the pawns upon which Kramnik based his strategy will be crowned.

TIP: A broad centre (three or more pawns) can offer your pieces excellent shelter, can close out the opponent's pieces and has the long-term potential to later create dangerous promotion threats.

Game 49
□ Leko ■ Zvjaginsev
Wijk aan Zee 1995

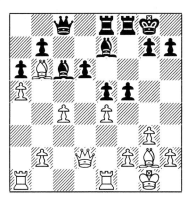 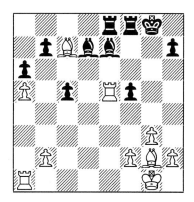

Diagram 5
Black's d6-pawn is weak

Diagram 6
Black still has weaknesses

This time the pawn structures are more or less defined, with the backward d-pawn a target and White enjoying a sort of mini (3-2) pawn majority on the queenside. However, after 19 exf5?! Bxg2 20 Kxg2 Qxc4 21 Rac1 Qb5, for example, Black's chances are preferable. Furthermore, the pawns on d6 and e5 might later be transformed to an attacking force. With this in mind White, to move, has the power to drastically alter the terrain, forcing a favourable break-up of Black's pawns.

19 Bh3! g6

Black opts to keep his light-squared bishop in the game. The variation 19...Bd7 20 Bxf5 Bxf5 21 exf5 Qxc4 22 Rac1 Qb5 23 Rc7 is crucially different to the one in the previous note since White's rook stands on the seventh rank.

20 exf5 gxf5 21 c5!

The point. Black's initially solid pawns are under severe pressure and, suddenly, are in danger of parting company.

21...Qe6

Too accommodating is 21...dxc5 22 Rxe5.

22 Bc7!

After 22 cxd6 Bxd6 23 Rad1 Bb8 Black's centre pawns remain intact.

22...dxc5 23 Rxe5!

23 Bxe5? Rd8! 24 Qf4 Qd5 is an unwelcome turnaround. The text, however, practically forces simplification into a very promising ending in which Black suffers from weak pawns.

TIP: Divide and conquer.

23...Qd7

23...Qg6 24 Rae1 Bg5 25 f4 is even worse.

24 Qxd7 Bxd7 25 Bg2! (Diagram 6)

Black simply has more weaknesses than his opponent, with b7, c5 and f5 all liabilities. Again the defender's problems increase with the number of pawn islands.

25...Bf6!

A nice try. 25...Bc6? 26 Bxc6 bxc6 27 Rae1, on the other hand, ends the game.

26 Rxe8 Rxe8 27 Bxb7 Bb5!

Black cannot let the a-pawn go, e.g. 27...Bxb2 28 Rb1 Bd4 29 Bxa6 etc.

28 Rc1! Bg5!?

Again Black makes the most of his chances. 28...Bxb2 29 Rxc5 Re1+ 30 Kg2 Bf1+ 31 Kf3 merely checks White's king up the board.

29 Bf4!

Everything has a price, and in this case White accepts structural damage of his own rather than walk into 29 Rxc5? Re1+ 30 Kg2 Bf1+ 31 Kf3 Be2+ 32 Kg2 Bf1+ with a draw.

29...Bxf4 30 gxf4 c4 31 Bd5+ Kg7 32 Bxc4 Rc8 33 b3 Rc5 34 Kg2 Bxc4

34...Bc6+ 35 Kg3 Rxa5 36 Re1! is easy for White.

35 bxc4

The ending is winning for White. The game ended as follows: **35...Kf7** (35...Rxa5 36 c5 Rb5 37 c6 Rb8 38 c7 Rc8 39 Kg3 Kf7 40 Kh4 Ke7 41 Rc6 Kd7 42 Rxa6 Rxc7 43 Kg5) **36 Kg3 Rxa5 37 c5 Ke7 38 Kh4! h6 39 Rc4!** (39 Kh5? Ra4 40 Kxh6 Rxf4) **39...Rb5** (39...Kd7 40 c6+ Kc7 41 Kh5 Ra2 42 Kxh6 Rxf2 43 h4) **40 Kh5 a5 41 c6 Kd8 42 Kxh6 Rb4 43 Rc2 a4** (43...Rxf4 44 Kg5 Rf3 45 h4) **44 Kg5 a3 45 h4 Rb2 46 Rc3 a2 47 Ra3 Kc7 48 Ra6 Rxf2 49 h5 Rh2 50 h6 1-0**

It is no coincidence that White's endeavours to inflict structural punishment on his opponent soon resulted in the makings of a decisive advantage, all the play revolving around Black's vulnerable pawns.

WARNING: Every pawn move can potentially create weaknesses. Advance them with care!

The Power of the d-pawn

The d-pawn – especially in White's hands – seems to have a mysterious hidden power capable of leaving the opponent in terrible trouble. Its mere presence can make life uncomfortable, yet even when it can be captured the implications can be catastrophic for the defender...

Game 50
□ **Kramnik** ■ **Anand**
Las Palmas 1996

After the opening moves **1 Nf3 Nf6 2 c4 b6 3 g3 Bb7 4 Bg2 e6 5 0-0 Be7 6 Nc3 0-0 7 Re1 d5 8 cxd5 Nxd5 9 e4 Nxc3 10 bxc3 c5 11 d4 Nd7 12 Bf4 Nf6 13 Ne5! cxd4 14 cxd4 Bb4 15 Re3 Rc8** the following position was reached:

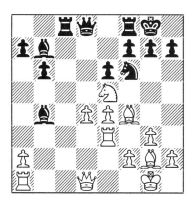

Diagram 7	**Diagram 8**
White has an extra centre pawn	White has a big d-pawn!

Both sides have decently posted pieces and a sound pawn structure. Clearly White has ambitions to make something of his extra centre pawn and, in fact, he sets about doing so immediately.

16 d5!

Normally this would simply lose a pawn but, having seen his rook evicted from e1, White can afford the luxury of early middlegame aggression because this piece is ready to nudge to the d-file if necessary.

16...exd5

A couple of tries with the advanced bishop need to be checked. First 16...Bc3 17 Nc6! Bxc6 18 Rxc3 exd5 19 exd5 cannot be met with 19...Bxd5? 20 Rxc8 Qxc8 21 Bxd5 Rd8 because White replies 22 Rc1!, e.g. 22...Qd7 23 Bxf7+ Kxf7 24 Rc7 Qxc7 25 Qb3+ etc. Hitting the other rook again with 16...Bc5 17 Rd3 Ba6 18 Rd2 Bb4 leads to an advantage to White after 19 Nc6 Rxc6 20 dxc6 Bxd2 21 Qxd2, when White has the bishop pair and the d-pawn has been promoted to a passed c-pawn (a common occurrence in such situations).

17 exd5 Bd6

Sensible play from Anand. Foolhardy for Black is 17...Nxd5 18 Rd3 Nxf4 (18...Rc5 19 Be3 Rb5 20 a4 Ra5 21 Nc4) 19 gxf4, e.g. 19...Bxg2 20 Rxd8 Rfxd8 (20...Rcxd8 21 Qb3) 21 Qb3 Bc3 22 Kxg2! Bxa1 23 Nxf7 Kf8 24 Ng5 Rd7 25 Qe6, or 19...Qc7 20 Rd7 Rfd8 21 Rxc7 Rxd1+ 22 Rxd1 Rxc7 23 Rd8+ Bf8 24 Bxb7 Rxb7 25 Nd7 Rxd7 26 Rxd7 a5 27 Rb7. Also poor is 17...Bxd5 18 Rd3 Bxg2 19 Rxd8 Rfxd8 (19...Rcxd8 20 Qb3) 20 Qb3 and Black is clearly worse, while 17...Bc5 18 Rd3 Ba6 19 Rd2 Bb4 again runs into 20 Nc6.

These lines illustrate the problems Black can have when faced with a rampant d-pawn in these positions.

18 Nc6 Bxc6 19 Bxd6

19 dxc6 Bxf4 20 gxf4 Qxd1+ 21 Rxd1 Rc7 is equal.

19...Ba4

This time 19...Qxd6 20 dxc6 Qxd1+ 21 Rxd1 sees White, compared with the previous note, keep his kingside pawns intact, enabling him to create play on a second front, e.g. 22 f4 Rfc8 23 Bf3 Kf8 24 g4 h6 25 h4 etc. Instead Black is happy to slightly complicate matters.

20 Bxf8!?

Not strictly necessary since 20 Qxa4 Qxd6 21 Qxa7 Nxd5 (21...Ra8 22 Qe7) 22 Bxd5 Qxd5 23 Qxb6 nets White a safe pawn. Note that this line is a great deal better than 22 Rd1??, which loses to 22...Nxe3, and preferable to 22 Rd3, allowing 22...Qe5. However, as a favour to us, Kramnik opts instead to allow his d-pawn to take centre stage, even if this means letting the queen leave the theatre altogether.

20...Bxd1 21 Be7 Qc7

21...Nxd5? 22 Bxd8 (22 Rxd1? Qxe7) 22...Nxe3 23 Bg5 Nxg2 24 Rxd1 would be an amusing finish.

22 Rxd1 (Diagram 8) 22...Nd7 23 Bh3 h6 24 Bf5!?

Improving the bishop, monitoring the flight square on h7 and guarding the c2-square, but the chief merit of this move is to put the onus on Black to find a decent reply with the three pieces he has left.

24...b5?

24...Qb7 25 Bb4!? is the lesser evil, when White's larger army – of which the d-pawn is a key member – makes the game easier to conduct for Kramnik.

25 Bb4! Rd8 26 Re7 Qc4

26...g6 27 Be6!? (27 d6) 27...fxe6 28 dxe6 wins for White, e.g. 28...Qc2 29 Rdxd7 Qc1+ (29...Rxd7 30 exd7 Qd1+ 31 Kg2 Qd5+ 32 f3 Qxa2+ 33 Kh3) 30 Kg2 Qc6+ 31 Kh3 (the seventh rank!), or the less exciting but nonetheless dismal 28...Nc5 29 Rxc7 Rxd1+ 30 Kg2 Nxe6 31 Rxa7.

27 Rxd7! Rxd7 28 Bxd7 Qxb4 29 d6 (Diagram 9)

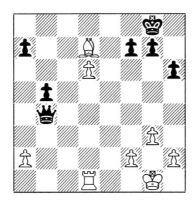
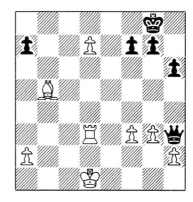

Diagram 9	**Diagram 10**
The passed pawn is well supported	The passed pawn lands

A rook, bishop and protected, supported passed pawn versus a queen!

29...Qa4

29...Qa5 30 Bc6 Kh7 31 d7 Qd8 fails anyway to 32 Re1 Qc7 33 Re8 etc.

30 Rd3

Also possible is 30 Re1!?, e.g. 30...Qd4 31 Bf5 g6 32 d7.

30...Qe4

30...Qxa2 31 Bf5 Qa5 32 d7 Qd8 33 Rc3, or 30...Qc4 31 Bf5 Qc1+ 32 Kg2 Qc6+ 33 f3 Qc2+ 34 Kh3 Qc5 35 Be4.

31 Bxb5 Qe1+ 32 Kg2 Qe4+ 33 Kg1 Qe1+ 34 Kg2 Qe4+ 35 Kf1 Qh1+ 36 Ke2 Qe4+ 37 Kf1 Qh1+ 38 Ke2 Qe4+ 39 Kd1! Qg4+.

39...Qh1+ 40 Kc2 Qa1 41 d7 Qxa2+ 42 Kd1 Qb1+ 43 Ke2 etc.

40 f3 Qh3

Or 40...Qb4 41 d7 Qb1+ 42 Ke2 Qxa2+ 43 Rd2 Qe6+ 44 Kf1 Qh3+ 45 Kg1.

41 d7 1-0 (Diagram 10)

D-pawn power!

Early queenside castling tends to make the d-pawn particularly dangerous. In the next example White employs a pawn break to release an ambitious d5-pawn and subsequently create an excellent outpost on d5.

Game 51
□ **Khenkin** ■ **Rogers**
Baden 1998

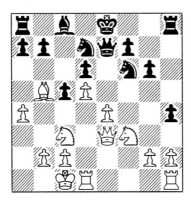

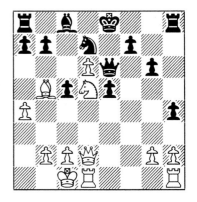

Diagram 11
White breaks through in the centre

Diagram 12
White's knight dominates

Black threatens to unpin his knight with....Kf8, after which he can take command of the e5-square.

15 e5!

Despite his apparent control of e5 Black is unable to capture the pawn, since 15...dxe5 16 d6 Qe6, for example, is awkward after 17 Ng5. Exploiting the pin on the e-file with 15...Kf8 serves only to invite the pawn to come to e6, so Black's next is both desirable and forced.

15...Ng4 16 Qd2 Ngxe5 17 Nxe5 dxe5 18 d6 Qe6 19 Nd5 (Diagram 12)

The point. The d-pawn not only cuts straight into Black's position but also makes way for an 'octopus' knight, which already threatens the fork on c7. Add to this the fact that the pawn is also passed and only two moves from glory, and White clearly has compensation for the sacrificed pawn.

19...Kf8

Unfortunately for Black the pawn is immune, as 19...Qxd6? 20 Bxd7+ Bxd7 21 Qg5 loses material.

20 Qg5! Rb8!

Thus far Black is handling the pressure well, avoiding 20...f6 21 Bxd7! fxg5 22 Bxe6 Bxe6 23 Nc7 and 20...Qxd6 21 Bxd7 Qxd7 22 Qf6! Rh5

23 Nc3. However, the d-pawn is the harbinger of doom for Black, who is no position to hold back the tide.

21 Nc7 Qf6

Tantamount to resignation. The outwardly aggressive 21...Qa2 is not enough to stave off defeat: 22 Bxd7 Bxd7 (22...Qa1+ 23 Kd2 Qxb2 24 Ne6+! Kg8 25 Bxc8) 23 Qe7+ Kg7 24 Qxd7 Rhd8 25 Qe7 Qa1+ 26 Kd2 Qxb2 27 Ne6+ Kg8 28 Rb1, or 24...Qa1+ 25 Kd2 Qxb2 26 Qb5! Qd4+ 27 Kc1 Qa1+ 28 Qb1 Qxa4 29 Qb2! etc.

22 Qxf6 Nxf6 23 d7 and after **23...Bxd7 24 Bxd7 Rd8 25 Bh3! Kg7 26 Rxd8! Rxd8 27 Rd1**

White went on to win the ending, the bishop being worth more than a couple of pawns...

The Pawn Break

Many players shy away from this aspect of the game because pawn breaks can be, by definition, rather complicated and difficult to anticipate, plan and, finally, evaluate.

Game 52
☐ **Hjartarson** ■ **Danielsen**
Akureyri 1994

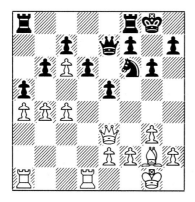

Diagram 13
How should White react?

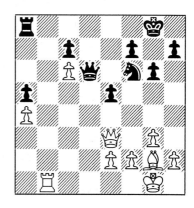

Diagram 14
The a5- and e5-pawns are weak

Too many club players would make sure that White's pawns remain 'intact' here and close the queenside with b4-b5. In fact there is an opportunity to break open the position by instead pushing the c-pawn:

19 c5!

Ideally the base of a pawn chain is the best to undermine, but we will settle for challenging both b6 and d6, a policy that subsequently puts pressure on a5 and e5.

19...bxc5?

The thematic pawn break induces a mistake from Black. Equally poor is 19...dxc5? 20 bxc5 Qxc5 21 Qxc5 bxc5 22 Rab1 Rab8 23 Rb7, but 19...axb4 20 cxd6 cxd6 is an improvement, although White enjoys the better prospects after 21 Qb3.

20 bxc5 Rfd8

20...dxc5 21 Rac1 Rfd8 22 Rxd8+ Rxd8 23 Qc3! exploits Black's broken pawns.

21 cxd6 Rxd6 22 Rxd6 Qxd6 23 Rb1 (Diagram 14)

By instigating a change in the respective structural layouts White has earned himself a clear advantage thanks to his opponent's more vulnerable pawns on a5 and e5.

TIP: (Long-range) Bishops tend to be superior to knights when working with major pieces to attack weaknesses.

23...h5 24 h3 e4

Closing out the bishop, but White is able to hold the c6-pawn, hit the a5-pawn and snare the e4-pawn.

25 Qc3 Kh7

What else? White intends to step up a gear by planting his rook on b5, and 25...Ra6? fails to 26 Bxe4!, exploiting the weak back rank – something Black now addresses.

26 Qc4 Qe7?!

26...Kg7 27 Bxe4 Nxe4 28 Qxe4 is the suggested improvement, when Black is a pawn down for nothing.

27 Rb5 h4

Just as White begins to turn the screw Black gives ground, although something is sure to give in this kind of position, with White being able to improve and Black short of 'waiting' moves.

28 g4 Rd8 29 e3 Rd1+ 30 Bf1 Ne8 31 Rxa5 f5 32 Rd5 Nd6?

Another, more serious mistake, in a hopeless situation. Instead 32...Rxd5 33 Qxd5 Nf6 34 Qc4 fxg4 35 a5 justifies White's initial break.

33 Rxd1 1-0

(33...Nxc4 34 Rd7).

Because pawn breaks can radically alter the general framework of a position the results tend to have long-term effects, the rest of the game often revolving around new structural features. However, these thematic pawn breaks are by their nature predictable in that, regardless of how well we might evaluate them, we include them in our calculations (in varying degrees of detail), nonetheless.

The 'shock' pawn break, on the other hand, is a different animal again, as the example below demonstrates.

Game 53
□ **Dragomaretsky** ■ **M.M.Ivanov**
Moscow 1995

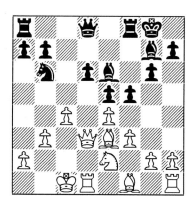

Diagram 15
Has White got control?

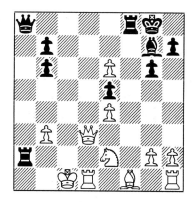

Diagram 16
White's king has been ripped open

Believing that his grip on the position is unshakeable White has just castled long. Wrong!

14...fxe4 15 fxe4 d5!!

Actually seeing this move played out on a board – and playing through the variations that follow – suggests that it is quite logical, but I doubt many strong players would, in fact, have factored the thrust into their calculations.

16 Bxb6

16 cxd5 Nxd5 17 exd5 Rc8+ is the main idea behind the break, opening lines of attack against White's king, e.g. 18 Nc3 e4, 18 Kd2 Qa5+ 19 Nc3 e4 and 18 Kb1 Bf5. White's choice in the game removes the knight but opens the a-file.

16...axb6 17 cxd5

17 exd5 Rxa2!, e.g. 18 dxe6 Qg5+ 19 Kb1 (19 Rd2 Bh6) 19...e4.

17...Rxa2! 18 dxe6

White's days are numbered after 18 Nc3 Qa8 19 Nxa2 Qxa2 20 Qe3 (20 Rd2 Bh6) 20...Rc8+ 21 Bc4 Bf8 etc.

18...Qa8!! (Diagram 16)

The '!!' are Ivanov's own, but he deserves considerable credit for the brutal change of events. At the moment White is a mere piece up, which amounts to less than the material about to be lost.

19 Qc3 Ra1+! 20 Kc2 Qa2+ 21 Qb2 Qxb2+ 22 Kxb2 Rxd1 23 e7

23 Ng3 Rf2+.

23...Re8

Black emerges with a clear exchange for no compensation.

24 Nc3 Rd2+ 25 Ka3

25 Kc1 Bh6.

25...Bf6! 26 Bc4+ Kg7 27 g3 Ra8+ 28 Kb4 Bxe7+ 29 Kb5 Bc5 30 b4 Rb2! 0-1

WARNING: Learn to always expect the unexpected – even from a lowly pawn!

Sacrificing a Piece for Pawns

Game 54
□ R.Leyva ■ Moreno
Las Tunas 1996

How much faith do you have in your centre pawns?

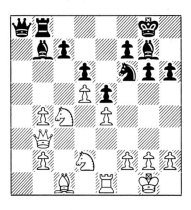

Diagram 17
How can Black blow up the centre?

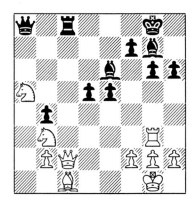

Diagram 18
Black has strong mobile pawns

Looking at Diagram 17 I could also ask: How annoying are White's centre pawns? Well, they close out the b7-bishop and the rather oddly placed queen, while their blockade of the pawns on d6 and e5 contributes to the locking in of Black's other bishop. Usually Black would like to challenge the d5-pawn with his c-pawn, but then the d6-pawn would be left unprotected.

18...Nxe4!

An excellent idea that not only removes the cause of Black's discomfort but also announces a kind of role reversal since White is about to find himself under pressure.

19 Rxe4

19 Nxe4? Bxd5 20 Qd3 Bxe4 21 Rxe4 d5 22 Re1 dxc4 23 Qxc4 is level, but 20...Rxb4! 21 Ncd2 f5 22 Nc3 Rd4 23 Qf1 Bxg2! is clearly better for Black.

19...Bxd5 20 Rg4 Be6 21 Rg3 d5 22 Na5 c5 23 Qc2 cxb4 24 Ndb3

Not 24 Nc6? Rb7 25 Nb3 Rc7 26 Nba5 Qxa5.

24...Rc8 (Diagram 18)

Black has two pawns for his piece but, more importantly, his mobile centre pawns are ready to advance, the rook has a new open file and the bishop pair looks impressive. Furthermore, White's rook, having come to g3 to defend the g2-pawn, is doing very little, while the knights also appear to be quite 'dim'. This does not necessarily mean that Black has an advantage, rather that his prospects are healthy.

25 Qd1 Qb8

Perhaps the most consistent treatment of the theme is to immediately advance the now unfettered pawns, e.g. 25...d4!? 26 Bd2 e4 27 Bxb4 d3 28 Ba3 Rc2 etc. Then Black might follow up by posting his bishop on e5 and launching the f-pawn.

26 h4 h5 27 Bd2 d4 28 Qe1 Rc2 29 Bxb4 Rxb2 30 Ba3 Ra2 31 Qc1 Qb5!

Black's forces enjoy far more harmony than White's and there is the constant threat to push the pawns. Note also that Black has no weaknesses. It is safe to say, then, that Black now has an advantage.

32 Be7 Rxa5?!

The knights just look clumsy whereas Black's rook is strong, so this trade must be wrong. In fact 32...d3! is a fitting culmination of Black's play thus far: 33 Qc5 Qxc5 34 Bxc5 e4 35 Bb4 Bxb3 36 Nxb3 Rb2 37 Re3 f5.

33 Nxa5 Qxa5 34 Ra3 Qd5 35 Qc7 Kh7 36 Qb8 Qe4??

Again the pawns offer the best chance, 36...d3! 37 Ra8 f5 38 Bf6 Bxf6

39 Ra7+ Bg7 being different to the game continuation since 40 Qf8 can be met with 40...Bd7, and in reply to 40 Qc7 Black has 40...Bf7 41 Qxf7 Qxf7 42 Rxf7 e4, e.g. 43 Kf1 Kg8 44 Rd7 Bh6 with equality.

37 Ra8 f5 38 Bf6! Bxf6

38...Qe1+ 39 Kh2 Qxf2 40 Qh8+! is a mate worth remembering!

39 Ra7+ Bg7 40 Qf8 1-0

Summary

Respect your pawns!

Structural weaknesses tend to have long-term significance

Consider the implications of pawn breaks

Don't be afraid to sacrifice a piece to release mobile, influential centre pawns

Chapter Six

Further Ideas

This chapter deals with several important issues, including where we should and should not post our pieces, the price of an outpost, the spiralling complexity of multiple exchanges and adapting to new circumstances. The games are intended to demonstrate the difficulty with which strong players make decisions in this or that aspect of the middlegame. For example, I have deliberately placed a game that centres around the use of a single square in the same chapter as examples of end-to-end action. This is because it is possible to create problems for the opponent by various means and, equally, it is just as easy to find yourself struggling against a 'dull' player as it is to be blown away by the club hacker if you are ill prepared for the numerous directions a game can take.

Creating and Using Outposts

Game 55
☐ **M.Gurevich** ■ **Kazhgaleyev**
Cappelle la Grande 1996

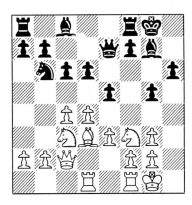

Diagram 1
How can White get hold of f5?

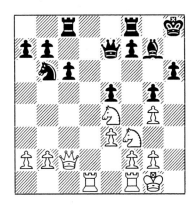

Diagram 2
White's control is worth a pawn

It does not take long to spot the weak square in Black's position – f5. Remember that all pawn moves create potential weaknesses, and in this case chasing White's bishop from g5 to h4 to g3 has resulted in a hole on f5.

15 dxe5!?

A theoretical novelty, this idea seems preferable to 15 b4 f5! 16 dxe5 dxe5 17 e4 fxe4 18 Nxe4 Qxb4 19 Nd6 Bg4 20 Qe2 Nd5 21 cxd5 cxd5, which has been assessed as unclear but looks good for Black. White aims to make full use of f5, hoping to install a piece in the heart of Black's kingside.

15...dxe5 16 Bh7+

Not 16 b3 f5, when Black's united front of pawns secures an advantage.

16...Kh8 17 Bf5!

White judges that the positional plus afforded him by control of f5 is worth the price of the c-pawn.

17...Nxc4

In the event of 17...Bxf5 18 Qxf5 Nxc4 White plays 19 Ne4 with the intention of practically ending the game after 20 Nexg5. Therefore Black might play 19...Qe6 20 Qxe6 fxe6 21 b3 Nb6, although 22 Nc5 leaves White with the advantage.

18 Bxc8 Raxc8 19 Ne4 Nb6

19...Qb4?! 20 a3 Qb5 21 Rc1.

20 g4! (Diagram 2)

Clamping down on f5 and paving the way for the knight to drop back to g3. If White can conduct the game in such a way that his kingside grip keeps Black under long-term pressure, then the pawn deficit will be irrelevant.

20...Rcd8

Of course White is ready for 20...Qe6? 21 Rd6! Qxg4 22 Rxh6+! Bxh6 23 Nf6.

21 b3!

Patient play, rather than the hasty 21 Ng3?! Qe6, hitting g4 and a2.

21...Rd5

Again 21...Qe6? fails, this time to 22 Nexg5! hxg5 23 Nxg5 Qg6 24 Qxg6 fxg6 25 Rxd8 Rxd8 26 Nf7+ etc.

22 Ng3! Rfd8

By now Black might as well forget about putting his queen on e6, since now 22...Qe6 meets with 23 e4! Rxd1 24 Rxd1 Qxg4 25 Nf5, investing a second pawn to leave Black's pieces severely lacking cohesion.

 TIP: A positional sacrifice, being long-term in nature, can be confusing for the opponent to handle since there tends to be no specific threats.

23 Nf5 Qd7

23...Qe6 24 e4 Rxd1 25 Rxd1 Rxd1+ 26 Qxd1 Qd7 27 Qxd7 Nxd7 28 Nd6 is good for White, but 26...Nd7 27 Qd6!? is less clear. The text challenges the d-file but perhaps this is not an important factor in view of what happens in the game.

24 Rc1 Qe6 25 e4 Rd3 26 Rfd1 Qd7 27 Re1 f6

27...Nc8 28 Qe2 Ne7 29 Ne3! Ng6 30 g3 seems like a long journey for the knight with no entry point available, and White has the attractive plan of Kg2 followed by bringing a rook to the h-file. Note that it is the availability of the f5-square rather than its occupation that is important to White.

28 Qe2!

Defending the knight in preparation for the g3, Kg2 and Rh1 plan.

28...a5

Black gets to work on the queenside, the area of the board where he has an extra pawn and where White is less able to defend, being busy with the game-plan on the other flank.

29 g3 a4 30 Kg2!? (Diagram 3)

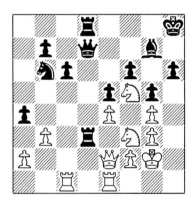
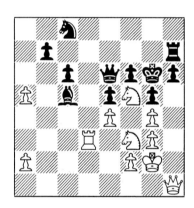

Diagram 3
The position is balanced

Diagram 4
White's pressure is overwhelming

30...Kh7

30...axb3 31 axb3 Rxb3 32 Red1 Rd3 33 Rh1 Kh7 34 Rxh6+ Bxh6 35 Rh1 has been evaluated as unclear by Gurevich but 35...Qf7 36 Nxh6 Qc4 37 Nf7+ Kg7 38 Nxd8 Rxd8 39 Qb2 Qb5 looks good for Black. However, 34 Qa2, denying Black the g8-flight square, renews the threat of Rxh6+.

31 Rh1 Kg6 32 Qe1!

Toying with ideas involving Rxh6+ and threatening Qb4.

32...Rh8

32...axb3 lets White have his fun: 33 Rxh6+! Bxh6 34 Qh1 Kf7 35

Nxe5+! fxe5 36 Qh5+! Kg8 37 Qxh6 with Rh1 to follow.

33 Qb4! Nc8 34 bxa4!?

A strange move, but White keeps his queen active and pushing the new a-pawn might prove awkward for Black.

34...Bf8 35 Qb1 Rh7

Offering extra protection to the b-pawn (another reason why White played 34 bxa4). Note how White's threats down the h-file and the subsequent opening of a second front of attack on the queenside have led to a certain untidiness among Black's pieces.

36 a5 Ba3 37 Rcd1 Rxd1 38 Rxd1 Qe6 39 Rd3! Bc5 40 Qh1 (Diagram 4)

None of this would be possible without the horse on f5!

40...h5 41 gxh5+ Kf7

41...Rxh5 42 Qxh5+ Kxh5 43 Ng7+ is a nice justification of White's strategy.

42 h6 Ne7 43 Qh5+ Ng6 44 Rb3 Qd7 45 N3h4! gxh4 46 Nxh4 1-0

The Colour Complex

Often associated with opposite-coloured bishop scenarios, concentrating exclusively on a colour complex is not so unusual, and the rewards tend to be considerable.

Game 56
☐ **Browne** ■ **Maloney**
USA 1997

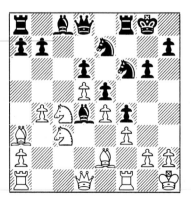

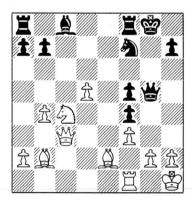

Diagram 5	**Diagram 6**
Black looks strong on the dark squares	Not any more!

With Black's bishop sitting right in the middle of the board, supported by a chain of pawns, it might be difficult to imagine that the dark squares are to be Black's undoing!

17 Nb5!

And so we begin...

17...Bxa1 18 Qxa1 Ne8 19 Nbxd6!!

White is concerned only with punishing his opponent on the dark squares rather than the 'points' value of his pieces.

19...Nxd6 20 Qxe5 Nf7

20...Ne8 21 b5 is interesting, e.g. 21...Kf7 22 d6 Ng8 23 Nb6! Be6 24 Nxa8 Qxa8 25 d7, or 21...Rf7 22 Bb2 Nf6 23 d6 Nf5 24 exf5 Bxf5 25 Nd2! threatening 26 Bc4. The general problem for Black is the continued suffering on the dark squares after returning material – if only because Black is so preoccupied shoring up the dark squares that he is ill equipped to address other areas.

21 Qc3 Nf5 22 exf5 gxf5 23 Bb2 Qg5 (Diagram 6)

For the moment Black defends the terribly weak spots on g7 and h8, but White's next prepares to bring support to the powerful queen and bishop.

24 Rg1! Rd8 25 g3 Kf8 26 gxf4 Qh6 27 b5!

Not satisfied with one set of dark squares, White switches to another with decisive effect. Black is unable to defend.

27...Rxd5 28 Ba3+ Ke8 29 Qb4

A nice finishing touch. White has dominated almost every dark square since embarking on his instructive mission!

29...Qe6 30 Qf8+ Kd7 31 Rg7 1-0

Piece Placement

The sensible positioning of your pieces in a game is vitally important. Just as you would not expect to see five or six members of a soccer team tucked away in a corner of the playing field, and therefore unable to make a worthwhile contribution to the game, nor does it make sense to treat pieces (and pawns) in the same manner in a game of chess! The biggest mistake is to neglect the king, but putting (or leaving) a piece in potential danger can be equally unwise.

Game 57
☐ **Gligoric** ■ **Z.Ilincic**
Yugoslavia Ch 1997

We have a reasonably normal position in which White has succeeded in achieving the traditionally desirable control of the square in front of the enemy isolated pawn. However, Black also has two pieces that monitor the d4-square, and the fact this his rook stands on the same, albeit closed file as White's queen affords the second player an interesting possibility.

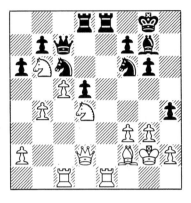

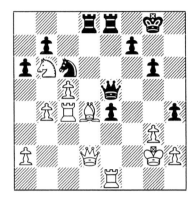

Diagram 7
White seems to have control

Diagram 8
Now the situation is less clear!

25...Ne4!!

Forking the queen and bishop and therefore forcing White to walk into an uncomfortable pin.

26 fxe4 dxe4 27 Rc4 Bxd4 28 Bxd4

28 Rxd4 leads to a rook ending that is very good for Black after 28...Nxd4 29 Bxd4 Qe5 30 Bxe5 (30 Rd1 e3) 30...Rxd2+ 31 Kh3 Rxe5 32 Nc4 Rdd5 33 Nxe5 Rxe5 etc.

28...Qe5! (Diagram 8)

A nice move to make. Thanks to his king White continues to suffer from awkwardly placed pieces.

29 Bxe5

Forced as 29 Rd1 e3 is much worse, e.g. 30 Bxe5? Rxd2+ 31 Rxd2 exd2 and the pawn cannot be caught.

29...Rxd2+ 30 Kh3 Rxe5 31 Rcxe4

Not 31 gxh4 e3 32 a4 e2.

31...Rxe4 32 Rxe4 hxg3 33 hxg3 Rxa2 and Black eventually took the full point.

WARNING: Beware an enemy rook on the same file as your queen!

When playing through the previous game you might have noticed that

White's knight on b6 failed to contribute to the cause thanks to its distant posting on b6.

TIP: An outpost in the opponent's half of the board is not always desirable.

This is demonstrated in the next game, when White fails to resist temptation.

Game 58
□ **Golubovic** ■ **Sveshnikov**
Bled 1996

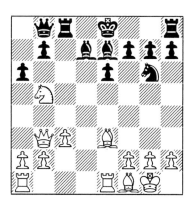
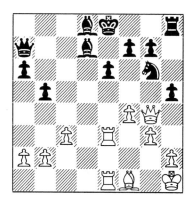

Diagram 9
Where should the knight go?

Diagram 10
Black gains time

Black has just nudged his a-pawn forward, giving White two main choices as to where to put the knight: the sensible d4-square or the adventurous a7.

17 Na7?

I must admit that there is a part of me that would spend an unreasonably long time weighing up the merits of this impudent move only to decide it is unwise – and then play it anyway! This is all the more impractical when the perfectly reasonable d4-square is available.

17...Rc5!

Whoops! Taking the rook leaves the stranded knight deservedly unprotected, so White's next is forced.

18 Qb6 Rh5 19 g3 Bd8!

Uncompromising play from Black that soon forces White to lose touch with the knight.

20 Qd4

20 Qb4 b6 21 a4 Qxa7 22 a5 Qb7 23 axb6 Ne5 is clearly better for Black.

20...b6 21 Qg4 Re5!?

21...Ra5 looks greedy but could be stronger, although the text guarantees Black a near decisive advantage.

22 f4 Rxe3 23 Rxe3 Qxa7

Every Russian schoolboy knows that two minor pieces beat a rook...

24 Rae1 b5 25 Kh1 h5! (Diagram 10)

It is no coincidence that part of the price White paid for unwisely venturing into enemy territory and subsequently trying to hang on to the wandering knight is the harassment of the queen. The latest gains time to launch an attack on White's king which, incidentally, has become exposed as a result of White's initial mistake.

26 Qd1 h4 27 f5 hxg3! 28 Rxg3 Qf2 0-1

A nice finish is 29 Rg2 Bc6 30 fxg6 Rxh2+! 31 Kxh2 Qh4+ 32 Kg1 Bb6+.

 WARNING: Don't lose touch with your pieces!

Game 59
☐ **V.L.Ivanov** ■ **Rodin**
Russia 1994

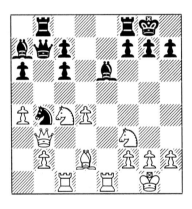

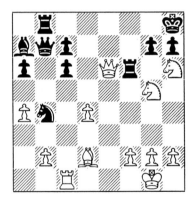

Diagram 11	**Diagram 12**
Black's pieces have wandered away	Black's pieces remain onlookers

 TIP: Make a conscious effort to keep a minimum number of pieces within defensive range of your king.

(Diagram 11) This is a good piece of advice with which Black is not acquainted in the diagram position, the sole protector being the bishop. With the exception of this piece and the rook, Black's forces are huddled on the queenside. Moreover, apart from possibilities on the b-file, it is difficult to understand what Black has been trying to achieve in the play leading up to the diagram position. As for White, his centrally located pieces afford him the opportunity to exploit his opponent's awkward placement.

1 Rxe6! fxe6 2 Na5! Qb6 3 Qxe6+ Kh8 4 Nc4!

Keeping Black's queen boxed in and preparing to send the knight to e5.

4...Qb7

Offering to return the exchange with 4...Rf6 leads to a good ending for White after 5 Qxf6 gxf6 6 Nxb6 Rxb6 7 a5! Rb5 8 Bxb4 Rxb4 9 Rxc6 Rxb2 (9...Bxd4 10 Nxd4 Rxd4 11 g3) 10 g3.

5 Nce5!

Suddenly White threatens 6 Ng6+!! hxg6 7 Qh3+ Kg8 8 Ng5 Rf5 9 Qh7+ Kf8 10 Qh8+ Ke7 11 Qxg7+ etc.

5...Rf6

Black might also challenge rather than attack the queen: 5...Qc8 6 Nf7+ Rxf7 (6...Kg8 7 Nh6+ Kh8 8 Qg8+) 7 Qxf7 Nd3 8 Rxc6 Rxb2 and now instead of the suggested 9 h3 White has 9 Rxc7 Rb1+ 10 Ne1 Qg8 11 Qf5! etc.

6 Nf7+ Kg8

Or 6...Rxf7 7 Qxf7 Nd3 8 Qf5!! Nxc1 9 Ng5 Ne2+ 10 Kf1 Kg8 11 Qxh7+ Kf8 12 Qh8+ Ke7 13 Qxg7+ Kd8 14 Qf6+ and White mates in two.

7 Nh6+ Kh8

7...Kf8 8 Qg8+.

8 Ng5!! 1-0 (Diagram 12)

Black's pieces remain rooted to the spot on the queenside and only the rook is witness to the impressive finish. White threatens 9 Qg8+! with a smothered mate and 8...Qc8 9 Ngf7+ Rxf7 10 Nxf7+ Kg8 11 Qc4! gives White a decisive material advantage.

Complex Situations

I began my chess writing career at the age of fifteen and this afforded me the early privilege of sitting around press rooms at top chess events, eating funny shaped sandwiches and occasionally watching strong players carry out an exhaustive post-mortem. The beauty of chess is that it can be simultaneously simple and complicated, and the next three games fall into the latter category!

Game 60
□ **Marin** ■ **Giorgadze**
Benasque 1996

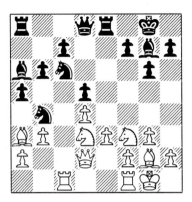
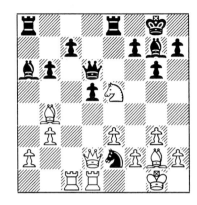

Diagram 13	**Diagram 14**
A tense position	White is in trouble

(Diagram 13) We have a standard position with decent development for both sides. Notice that a number of pieces can either capture or be captured, a feature that instigates a complex sequence of exchanges that requires the utmost care from both players.

17 Nxb4

With the more sound pawn structure White is happy to trade, hoping that his light-squared bishop and command of the c-file will prove effective.

17...axb4

17...Nxb4 18 Rfd1 Qd6 19 Ne1 and White unleashes the bishop and prepares to attack the pinned knight.

18 Rfd1 Qd6

After 18...bxa3 19 Rxc6 White's better pawns compensate for the bishop pair.

19 Ne5!?

19 Bb2 Bb5 20 Ra1 is about level but the text initiates complications that leave little room for error. We are less concerned with the soundness of White's plan than the manner in which these strong GMs handle the ensuing complexities. When playing through the following variations try to imagine how clearly you would calculate them during a game.

19...Nxd4

Black is happy to oblige, and this may well be the best move. 19...Bxe5 20 dxe5 Nxe5 21 Bxb4 c5 22 Bc3 Nd3 23 Rc2 d4 24 exd4 cxd4 25 Ba1 looks like White is being pushed back, but after sending his queen to h6 and nudging his rook from c2 to d2 White has the makings of an initiative. Sensible is 19...Nxe5 20 Bxb4 c5 21 dxe5 Bxe5 22 Bc3 with chances for both sides.

20 Bxb4

20 exd4 bxa3 21 Rc6 Qd8 leaves Black with a safe extra pawn.

20...Ne2+ (Diagram 14)

White is in danger of regretting his offer to liven up the game. Black's queen is attacked but this can be easily remedied by blocking with the c-pawn (once White's king moves out of check), which would then leave White's bishop under threat, along with his knight and rook! Having three pieces attacked simultaneously is not ideal, so White has little choice but to taste his own medicine.

21 Qxe2 Bxe2

White is happy to settle for the slight edge that follows 21...Qxb4 22 Nd3 Qd6 23 Qc2 etc.

22 Bxd6 Bxd1!

Stronger than 22...cxd6 23 Rd2.

23 Nxf7! (Diagram 15)

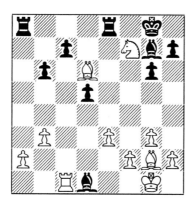
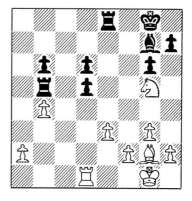

Diagram 15	Diagram 16
White is stirring up trouble	A double-edged position

23...cxd6!?

23...Kxf7 24 Bxd5+ Kf6 25 Rxd1 cxd6 26 Bxa8 Rxa8 27 Rxd6+ Kf7 28 a4 is unclear.

24 Ng5!

24 Bxd5? runs into 24...Bf3! with a decisive lead for Black.

24...Ra5

24...Bg4 25 Bxd5+ Kh8 (25...Kf8 26 Rc7) 26 Nf7+ Kg8 27 Ng5+ is a fair draw and 27 Nh6+ Kh8 28 Nxg4? Ra5! 29 Bc6 Rc8 30 b4 Rxa2 favours Black, but 24...Bxb3!? 25 axb3 needs analysing. 25...Ra1 26 Bxd5+ Kf8 27 Nxh7+ Ke7 28 Rxa1 Bxa1 29 Ng5 is fine for White, with two pawns for the exchange and good pieces. This leaves 25...Ra5 26 b4 Rb5 27 Bh3! Rxb4 28 Be6+. Now 28...Kf8? 29 Rc7 spells trouble, so perhaps Black should take the draw after 28...Kh8 29 Nf7+ Kg8 30 Ng5+.

25 b4

Yet another threat! 25 Rxd1 d4! loosens White up.

25...Rb5 26 Rxd1 (Diagram 16) 26...h6

Here 26...d4 27 Bc6 Rxg5 28 Bxe8 dxe3 29 f4 Rf5 30 Rxd6 cannot be recommended for Black, but how should White respond to the latest attack?

27 a3

Neither 27 Rb1?! hxg5 28 Bf1 Rc5! 29 bxc5 bxc5 nor 28 a4! d4 29 axb5 dxe3 appeal, but 27 a4 hxg5 28 axb5 d4 29 exd4 (29 e4 Rc8) 29...Re2 might prove difficult for Black. However, 27 Nh3! Rxb4 28 Bxd5+ Kh7 29 Nf4 makes a lot of sense, when 29...g5? 30 Nd3 embarrasses the rook in view of 30...Ra4 31 Bc6.

27...hxg5 28 Bf1 Rxb4 29 axb4 d4! 30 Bb5

In the event of 30 e4 Rxe4 (30...Ra8!?) 31 Bd3 Re7 32 Bxg6 Re2 the situation is less clear.

30...Re7 31 exd4 Re4 32 Kg2 ½-½

Considering the number of pieces attacked and captured, and at such a rate, a draw is a fair result. It would have been easy for either player to lose track of the 'score', miscalculate or make an incorrect evaluation during the complicated sequences.

The previous game saw a normal middlegame position turn into a bizarre series of captures and threats, but tactics took second place to ending considerations. Now we turn our attention to a super-heavyweight slugfest, featuring the world's number one and number two players.

Game 61
□ **Kasparov** ■ **Kramnik**
Novgorod 1994

Both queens are attacked, hence White's opening salvo!

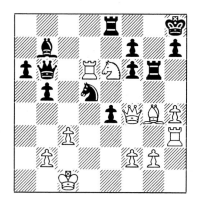

Diagram 17
Everything is *en prise*!

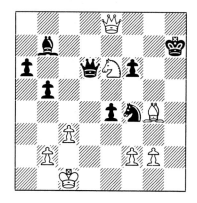

Diagram 18
White has a winning endgame

27 h5!!

Of course.

27...Nxf4

27...Rxg4 28 Qxg4 Rg8 29 Qxg8+ Kxg8 30 Rg3+ Kh8 31 Nd8! is nice, while 27...Rxe6 28 hxg6 wins for White after 28...fxg6 29 Qh6, or 28...Nxf4 29 Rxh7+ Kg8 30 gxf7+ Kf8 (30...Kxh7 31 Rxb6) 31 Rh8+ Kxf7 32 Bxe6+ Nxe6 33 Rxb6 etc.

28 hxg6 Qxd6

If 28...Rxe6 White replies 29 Rxh7+ and transposes to 27...Rxe6 in the previous note.

29 Rxh7+ Kg8 30 gxf7+ Kxh7 31 fxe8Q (Diagram 18)

Amazingly, after the smoke from the fireworks has cleared, White still has threats against Black's king that are enough to take the game to a winning ending.

31...Nxe6 32 Bf5+ Kg7 33 Qg6+ Kf8 34 Qxf6+ Ke8 35 Bxe6 Qf8

After 35...e3 36 fxe3 Bxg2 37 Bf7+ Kd7 38 Be8+ Kc7 39 Qg7+ Kd8 40 Qxg2 Kxe8 41 Qe4+! the queens are exchanged, while the alternative continuation 35...Bc6 36 Bf7+ Kd7 37 Be8+! leads to another decisive pawn ending.

36 Bd7+ 1-0

TIP: Study the games collections of the great attacking players and see how your analysis compares with theirs.

Finally a game in which White gets so clever he even confuses himself...

Game 62
□ Afek ■ M.Shrentzel
Tel Aviv 1993

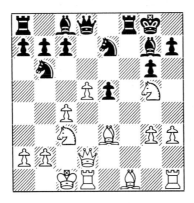

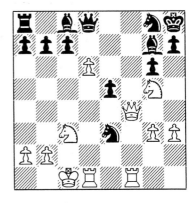

Diagram 19
A quiet position?

Diagram 20
Not any more!

14...Rxf1!

Black parts with his rook in order to snare both enemy bishops. However, White seems unconcerned with his opponent's plan.

15 Rhxf1 Nxc4 16 Qf2 Nxe3

16...Nf5!? closes the f-file but turns out to favour White after 17 Bd2 Nxd2 18 Qxd2 Nd4 19 Nf7 Qe7 20 Nh6+ Bxh6 21 Qxh6 etc.

17 Qf7+! Kh8 18 d6!?

Typical of IM Afek's tricky, gladiatorial style, this gives Black a couple of other things to worry about in addition to his weak back rank and ideas with Nf7+.

18...Ng8!

The downsides to this might be that Black ignores the d-pawn and sets himself up to be the victim of a smothered mate(!), but the alternatives are worse. 18...Nc6 19 dxc7 wins for White, while 18...cxd6 19 Rxd6! Bd7 20 Ne6 is awkward indeed, e.g. 20...Qg8 21 Rxd7 Nxf1 22 Qxe7 Bh6+ 23 Kb1, or 20...Bxe6 21 Rxd8+ Rxd8 22 Qxe7 Nxf1 23 Qxd8+ Bg8 24 Ne4 etc.

19 Qf4??! (Diagram 20)

This entertaining but unsound try is also to be expected of White, but the ostensibly sensible 19 Nce4!! actually hides a spectacular threat. 19...Nxd1?, for example, walks right into 20 Qxg7+! Kxg7 21 Rf7+ and mate next move. Meanwhile 19...Nxf1 20 dxc7! Qxd1+ (20...Qf8 21

Rd8!) 21 Kxd1 Ne3+ 22 Ke2 is good for White since 22...Nf5? meets with 23 Qxf5! and the smothered mate on f7 comes into play. Another try is 19...Nh6 20 dxc7 Qxd1+ 21 Rxd1 Nxf7, but then White has 22 Rd8+! etc.

Returning to the position after 19 Qf4??!, Black has a drastic way to address the threat of 20 Nf7 mate.

19...Qxg5!! 20 Qxg5 Nxf1!

Suddenly White is faced with the loss of his own queen on the h6-c1 diagonal, and he has already invested material!

21 Rxf1 (Diagram 21)

21 Kb1 Bf5+ 22 Ka1 Bh6 23 Qh4 Ne3 24 Rd2 cxd6 is unpleasant for White, and 21 Kc2 Bf5+ 22 Kb3 Bh6 23 Qh4 Ne3 even worse – hence the text.

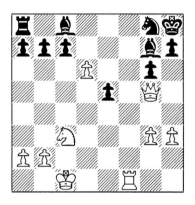

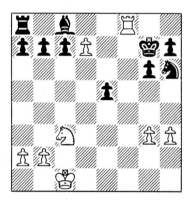

Diagram 21
Black has an obvious move...

Diagram 22
A final trick

21...Bh6?

It is precisely because this is difficult to resist that Black should investigate alternatives! 'The threat is stronger than its execution', they say, and this points to 21...Bxh3!?, adding White's rook to the hit list. Then 22 Kd1 Bxf1 23 dxc7 Bh3 24 Nd5 Be6 25 Qd8 Rc8 26 Ne7 has been assessed as good for White, but 26...Rxd8+ 27 cxd8Q Bf6! picks up the knight free of charge.

22 Qxh6 Nxh6 23 Rf8+ Kg7 24 d7! (Diagram 22)

The final 'trick' to take us to an ending.

24...Bxd7 25 Rxa8 Bxh3 26 Rxa7 Bg2 27 a4 Nf5 28 Ne2

This position is okay for Black, who has a good kingside majority, but after inaccurate play White eventually won.

Summary

Look for influential outposts

Be aware of the implications of operating on a specific colour complex

Don't neglect your king

Avoid awkward/illogical piece placement

Chapter Seven

Solutions to Exercises

Chapter 1

Exercise 1
☐ **A.Gunnarson** ■ **Hjartarson**
Deildarkeppni 1996

1...Nxf3+! 2 Bxf3 Nxe4 3 Bxe4 Rxe4+

So far so simple, but it gets more complex from here...

4 Ne3

4 Be3 meets with 4...Qe7!, e.g. 5 Kf2 Bb5 6 Re1 Re8 and White is tied up, or 5 Qxd7 Rxe3+ 6 Nxe3 Qxe3+ 7 Kf1 Qf3+ etc. Running with 4 Kf2 Qf6+ 5 Kg1 does not help in view of 5...Qf3 6 Ne3 Rxe3! 7 Rf1 (7 Bxe3 Bc6) 7...Re1! 8 Rxe1 Bc6.

4...Qg5 5 Qd5

5 Qc1 Bb2! 6 Qxb2 Qxc5, or 5 Rc1 Bf8! 6 Bxf8 Rxe3+ 7 Kf2 Qf5+! 8 Kg1 (8 Kxe3 Re8+ 9 Kd4 c5+ with mate on e4) 8...Qe4.

5...Rxe3+! 6 Kf2 Qf6+! 7 Kxe3 Re8+ 8 Kd3 Bb5+ 0-1

Exercise 2
☐ **Pinski** ■ **Twardowski**
Zagan 1995

1 Bxb5+! axb5 2 Ndxb5 Qe7 3 Nxd6+!

The point.

3...Qxd6 4 Qxf7+ Kd8 5 Rd1 Bd2 6 Rxd2!

Not 6 Bxc5?? Qxh2 mate!

6...Qxd2 7 Bxc5! Kc8

7...Qd7 8 Rd1 Bd5 9 exd5!? Qxf7 10 dxe6+ leaves White with a bishop and four(!) pawns for a rook.

8 Rd1 Qxd1+

After 8...Qh6 9 Qd7+ Kb8 10 Qd6+ Kc8 11 Bb6! Black cannot defend both c7 and d8.

9 Nxd1 Ra6 10 h3! and White emerges with a decisive material advantage.

Exercise 3
☐ **V.Ivanov** ■ **Hermlin**
Helsinki 1996

Black tried 5...Bg5?, when 6 Qh7+! Kf8 7 Rd7!! won for White after 7...Qxb3+ 8 axb3 a2+ 9 Kb2 Bf6+ 10 c3 Bg7 11 gxf7 Bxf7 12 Qd3! (defending e2) 12...b5 13 Qf3 Re7 14 Rxe7 Kxe7 15 Qxc6 1-0.

The simpler **5...Bf6!?** does more than hold for Black, e.g. 6 Rd7 Bg7 7 Qh7+ Kf8 8 gxf7 Bxd7 9 Qg8+ Ke7 10 fxe8Q+ Rxe8 11 Qxg7+ Kd8 12 Rd1 Qc7. Instead 6 g7?? Qxb3+!! 7 cxb3 Bf5+ 8 Kc1 Bb2+ 9 Kd2 Rad8+ leads to mate, while 6 Rhg1 Qxb3+!! 7 cxb3 Bf5+ 8 Rd3 Bxd3+ 9 Kc1 Bxg6 is final.

Exercise 4
☐ **Gdanski** ■ **Wallace**
Gothenburg 1996

Major pieces sharing a reasonably open line require close attention, and in this case Black is taken by surprise...

1 Rxf6!! gxf6 2 Bxf6+! Qxf6 3 Qg8+! Kxg8 4 Bd5+ 1-0

Chapter 3

Exercise 1
☐ **Matveeva** ■ **Sziebert**
Cappelle la Grande 1997

1...Rxf3!! 2 Nxc5

After 2 gxf3 Nxf3 all White's tries run into the same move:

a) 3 Ng4 Rd2!! 4 Nxd2 Nxd2+ 5 Kg1 Qxg4+.

b) 3 h3 Rd2!! 4 Nxd2 (4 Qf6 Qxh3+!) 4...Qg3 etc.

c) 3 Kg2 Rd2!! 4 Qf6 (4 Qc1 Qg4+ 5 Kh1 Qh3!) 4...Nxe1+ 5 Kg1 Qxf6 6 Nxf6+ Kf7 7 N2e4 (7 N6e4 Nf3+) 7...Rg2+! 8 Kh1 Re2 9 Rf4 Nd3 10 Rh4 Bxe4+ 11 Nxe4 Rxe4!.

2...Rdf8 3 Ncd3

Or 3 Kg1 Rg3! 4 Nfe4 (4 hxg3 Nf3+! 5 gxf3 Qxg3+) 4...Nf3+ 5 Rxf3 Rgxf3!.

3...Rg3 4 Rg1 Nf3! 0-1

All this was made possible by Black's bishop.

Exercise 2
☐ **Martinez** ■ **O.Martin**
Havana 1996

---

1 Bxe4! fxe4 2 f5!

Suddenly White's rooks come to life, the threat of 3 f6 forcing Black's next.

2...Nexf5 3 Rxf5+!!

Not 3 Rxe4? Kg8! 4 Ref4 Qe3! 5 Nxd6 (5 Rxf5 Qe4+!) 5...Ng3+ 6 Kg2 Nxf1.

3...Nxf5 4 Rxe4! Qc8 5 Re7+! 1-0

Exercise 3
□ **Serafimov** ■ **Dovramadjiev**
Bulgaria 1996

---

1 Bxf5! gxf5 2 Qg5+ Kh8

2...Kf7 3 Nxf5 Rxe1+ 4 Rxe1.

3 Nxf5

3 Rxe8!? also looks strong, but the game choice provides a better illustration of the power of the diagonal.

3...d4 4 N3xd4! Be5 5 Rxe5! Rxe5

5...cxd4 6 Rxe8.

6 f4! Re7

Or 6...Ree8 7 Nc6! Qf7 (7...Re6 8 Nce7!) 8 Ne5 Qg8 9 Nd7!.

7 Nf3 Re6 8 Ne5 Qc7 9 Ng4 Qf7 10 Nxf6 Rxf6 11 Re1 1-0

Black resigned in view of 11 Re1 Qg6 (or 11...Bc6 12 Re6!) 12 Bxf6+ Qxf6 13 Qxf6+ Rxf6 14 Re8+.

Exercise 4
□ **P.Popovic** ■ **D.Kosic**
Novi Sad 1992

---

1 g5! hxg5 2 Ng6!!

Exploiting the open h-file by both threatening mate on h8 and ruling out the blockading ...Rh4.

2...Nh7

After 2...fxg6 3 Qxe6+ Qf7 White has 4 Rh8+.

3 Rxh7! 1-0

Black resigned in view of 3...Kxh7 4 Qh5+ or 3...fxg6 4 Qxe6+ Kxh7 (4...Qf7 5 Rh8+) 5 Qxg6+ Kg8 6 Re8+.

Chapter 4

Exercise 1
□ **Pisseaux** ■ **O.Garcia**
Cuba 1997

1...e3!!

Most players would consider this move until noticing it leaves the queen unprotected!

2 Qxd3

a) 2 Rxe3 Qxd1+ 3 Rxd1 Rxb2.

b) 2 f3 Rd2! 3 Qc1 Qg6.

c) 2 Rf1 Qg6.

d) 2 Kh1 Bxg2+! 3 Kxg2 Rxf2+.

2...exf2+ 3 Kf1 Bxg2+!! 4 Kxg2 fxe1N+! 0-1

The mere presence of Black's rook is devastating.

Exercise 2
☐ **Legky** ■ **David**
France 1997

Yes.

1...Qxb4! 2 Nb5 Qxc4!!

2...Qa4? 3 Qxa4 Nxa4 4 Nxd6.

3 Qxc4 Bxb5 4 Qc3

4 Qc2 Nd3+ 5 Kd1 Ba4! 6 Qxa4 Nb2+.

4...Nfxe4!

The mate on f1 highlights White's plight on the light squares.

5 Qe3 Nd3+ 6 Kd1 Ba4+! 7 Ke2 Nf4+ 0-1

Black's investment is about to reap great rewards.

Exercise 3
☐ **Skatchkov** ■ **Mirkovic**
Palic 1995

1...Rg2! 2 Rxg2

After 2 Bd4 Reg8 Black brings the queen to g6.

2...hxg2+ 3 Kxg2

3 Kg1 Qh3 4 Qh2 Qxh2+ 5 Kxh2 Bxf3 and 3 Kh2 Rh8 4 Qh4 (4 Kxg2 Qg6+! 5 Qg3 Bxf3+!) 4...Rh7! 5 Kg1 Bg6 win for Black.

3...Qg6+! 4 Qg3

4 Kf1 Qd3+ 5 Kg2 (5 Ke1 Rg8 6 Qh2 Bxf3) 5...Rg8+, or 4 Kh2 Bxf3! 5 Qxf3 Rh8+ 6 Qh3+ Rxh3+ 7 Kxh3 Qd3+ and the d-pawn advances.

4...Bxf3+! 0-1

5 Kxf3 allows instant mate, 5 Kf1 Qd3+ 6 Kg1 Rh8 merely takes longer.

Exercise 4
☐ **Bezgodov** ■ **Berezjuk**
Minsk 1996

1 Qxg6+!

Combining themes, White has the opportunity to dominate on the dark squares.

1...hxg6 2 Bxe5 Qc6?

2...Re8? 3 Rh8+ Kf7 4 Rh7+ wins for White, while 2...Qh7 3 Rxh7 Kxh7 4 Bd4 is an awful ending for Black. However, 2...Qc8! 3 Rh8+ Kf7 4 Rh7+ Ke6 is Black's most accurate continuation, when 5 Bg7+ Kd6 6 Bxf8+ Qxf8 7 Rxb7 Qxf2 8 Ra1 favours White.

3 Rh8+ Kf7 4 Rh7+ Ke6

4...Ke8?? 5 Bf6+ is mate, and 4...Kg8?? 5 Rg7+ Kh8 6 Rxb7+ Rf6 fails to 7 Bxf6+ Qxf6 8 Re8+.

5 Bg7+ Kf5

5...Kf7 6 Bd4+ Kg8 7 Rg7+ is simple, but 5...Kd7 6 Bxf8+ Kc8 7 Bd6! demonstrates the influence of White's bishop.

6 Bxf8 d4

6...g5 7 Rf7+ Kg6 8 Rg7+ Kf5 9 Ree7 takes longer to lose, so Black at least gives his bishop a role.

7 Rf7+ Kg4 8 Re4+! Kh5 9 g4+ Kg5 10 Be7+ Kh6 11 g5+ 1–0